An Illustrated Guide to the
COMMONBIRDS of CAPECOD

PETER TRULL   ILLUSTRATIONS BY CATHERINE E. CLARK

Copyright © 2011 by Peter Trull
Illustrations Copyright © 2011 by Catherine E. Clark

Library of Congress Control Number: 2011931542

Designed by Justin Watkinson
Cover design by Bruce Waters
Type set in Futura Std/Minion Pro
ISBN: 978-0-7643-3877-9
Printed in China

Published by Schiffer Publishing, Ltd.
4880 Lower Valley Road
Atglen, PA 19310
Phone: (610) 593-1777; Fax: (610) 593-2002
E-mail: Info@schifferbooks.com

ACKNOWLEDGMENTS

It was Artist Cathy Clark who suggested we redo my 1991 edition of *A Guide to the Common Birds of Cape Cod* in a color format. Pete Schiffer at Schiffer Publishing was in agreement. He was also, as always, very patient with me. Thank you both. Andy Novak helped me pull this all together with his typing and transcription skills. A big thank you Andy! Support from my wife Carol is ongoing, it means so much.

In the older edition there was a page acknowledging the many people who brought that book from its original idea to a really popular teaching guide. There are friends that deserve repetition with special thanks. They are really much more than friends in my heart, having introduced me to the birds of Cape Cod in the 1970s: Vern Laux, Blair Nikula, Ian Nisbet, my mentor, and Dick Forster, God bless him

Today though, there is a whole bunch of folks, most of whom I've never met, who provide invaluable information to me and so many others, on a list serve called MASSBIRD.ORG. If you're not familiar with it, log on and subscribe. Every day I thank you all. For the most fun record keeping of every outing and birds spotted, log onto E-BIRD.ORG, the most amazing personal field notes, species records, and sighting location website imaginable. Thanks to the Cornell Lab of Ornithology and Marshall Iliff.

This book is dedicated to MIKE O'CONNOR
In Loving Memory of CASSIE MEECH

4880 Lower Valley Road Atglen, Pennsylvania 19310

CONTENTS

INTRODUCTION

My first book on this subject, *A Guide to the Common Birds of Cape Cod,* was printed in 1991, wow, twenty years ago. It taught thousands of people the joy, fun, excitement, and the learned skills of bird watching, or birding. The original edition has been reprinted three times. It had become a valued teaching guide, so we wanted to make it even better.

Here you'll find information added to the species accounts, including where to find many of them. The introduction has been lengthened to a chapter on how to see more birds and be a better birder, and the field trips have been lengthened to include more species. This is not a field guide for experienced or expert birders, although they may glean some valuable information about locations and logistics. Bird lovers, beginning birders who want to identify all those birds they're seeing or where to find birds on the cape, and folks who want to sharpen their birding skills will all find this book very useful.

Yes, larger, regional or national field guides are excellent, beautiful, and incredibly useful guides, but, with the sheer number of species described, the confusion for beginning birders, novice birders, or kids can be a limiting factor in their ability to learn and identify birds. If you are a beginner and are confused by all the choices, this guide will be a great help. Here you have a local guide that pretty much tells you what you are looking at. Take it with you, read it at home, learn as much as you can from it, use your binoculars, and most of all, love birds!

Peter Trull
December 2010

Okay, let's get right to the point. You want to be able to see and identify more birds. It's nice to know the local species, the "yard-birds." You see the robin on the lawn or the crow flying over. Maybe you see the Mourning Doves in the driveway, swallowing grit to help grind up seeds in their gizzard, or the raucous Blue Jay that seems to have 15 or 20 identical twins in the neighborhood.

Canada Geese are certainly known to everyone and seen at every large green space in town. How nice it was of us to create such immense and natural bird feeders for these "feathered cows" that flock to every green open space in town to graze. They used to migrate from the arctic to the southern marshes and farmlands, but golf courses, athletic fields, and parks put an end to that! Hey, why migrate when you can raise a family right next to a bird feeder of several acres!

Perhaps you have a bird feeder or two in your own yard, and you enjoy observing the birds as they come and go throughout the day. I throw seed on the ground and it works just fine. No geese, but lots of juncos, white-throats, towhees, and cardinals. But loose food thrown on the ground is not typical these days. The great diversity of feeders available at today's stores and specialty shops boggles the mind! Tube feeders, platforms, open or closed, window feeders, suet feeders, hummingbird feeders, and squirrel-proof feeders! Whew! There are people who have one of each!

With so many feeders, there's got to be a lot of birds! Well, that's right, there are lots of beautiful birds. Maybe you only get to look at the birds in the morning before work, or in the afternoon when your taking it easy, getting supper, or like me, doing dishes and watching the feeder from the kitchen window. It could be that you only pay attention to birds at your feeder on weekends when you have a little time. Whenever it is that you watch birds coming and going, remember that they have little regard for you. They are eating to survive. They fly from the window-side feeder right back to shelter, a protected place where they can crack open the black-oil sunflower seeds they carry in their beaks.

By feeding the birds, you are helping them survive. Do they need you? Not really. Are they dependent on you? Well, to a degree they are, because you are providing them with an easily accessible food source that they may certainly depend on to be there. Is it necessary to feed year round? Some people do and some people don't. It's really a matter of choice for you.

I generally stop around May 15, when the half-orange goes out on the deck rail as a treat for the orioles that are just getting back from the tropical jungle where they've been feeding with toucans! By then, the chickadees, titmice, nuthatches, and Downy Woodpeckers that have been chowing down on a variety of seeds and hammering on the beef suet all winter are quite capable of finding available, natural foods.

Still, some people like to have birds coming in all year and keep their feeders active. Whatever you decide, there is no wrong or right when it comes to feeding year round, no matter what the "experts" say. If you want to feed year-round, go right ahead; the birds will love it. Even though I don't feed in summer, I can remember more than once, seeing fluffy-headed fledgling chickadees coming in with mom or dad to the feeder platform whether there were seeds on it or not.

You and I both like birds and heaven knows there are lots of birds out there to observe. But why look at birds? What is this fascination with birds that is sweeping the country? Bird watching perches a close second to gardening as the number one pastime or hobby in the U.S. We watch birds because we can. They are all around us in a great, interesting variety, whether in the city or the country. We can attract them for close observation by using feeders and have the great pleasure of seeing these beautiful creatures and their colorful regalia of plumage up close!

So, we don't need to pretty picture books or nature shows on television. Everything we would read about or watch is right outside our window every day. Birds are so easy to find, and when you do it puts you in touch with the natural world in which we live. So let's get outside. Enter into any habitat you choose and you can find some birds and identify them! Shall we go to the woods, the fields or marsh, the open beach, a pond? Why not get on a boat and go out to sea! No matter where you go, you'll find birds and what fun it is to get to know them.

Binoculars Are a Must!

You must have an adequate pair of binoculars if you're going to watch birds. Now if you're saying "No, I can watch birds okay, I don't really need binoculars," return this book for a refund because the magnificent world of avifauna will never be opened to you without binoculars!

Believe me, there is a set of binoculars made just for you. They range from the lightest tiniest binoculars that fit into a shirt pocket to the heaviest cumbersome binocs that you would swear came from the wheelhouse of the Bismark!! You need to find the binoculars that feel most comfortable at your eyes.

Binoculars work best when you're looking through them. If you test binoculars at a store, don't look through a glass door to see how clear things look! The glass will distort the image. Get permission, then go out side and try several binocs until you find the best weight, power, and "handle-ability" (I just made that word up). Make sure that when you look though binoculars, you see a round circular image with no shadows or distortions. The more you use binoculars, the easier it is to see a clear view with no shadows.

Numbers on binoculars, like 7X, 8X, or 10x, describe the magnification. Usually, 7X is the best magnification for beginners, because the higher the magnification, the tougher it is to hold the binoculars steady without shake. A beginner birder would probably find it hard to hold or even see through a pair of 10X binoculars, but a person who's been birding for a few years may insist on having 10X.

On one of the eyepieces, you'll find numbers on each side of a center mark, along with a + or – (see diagram). This is for your own personal eye adjustment. Focus on an object using both eyepieces, as you would if you were looking at a bird. Look at a tree or license plate, something sharp. Close the eye without the adjustment numbers so that you're using one eye and looking through the eyepiece with the adjustment numbers on it. Now, turn the eyepiece with the numbers until the most absolute, sharpest image is found. At that point, determine where the lines are in relation to the numbers or plus and minus scale, that is where you should set that eyepiece lined up for maximum clarity for your eyes, all the time.

The number on the other side of the X on binoculars, —X40, describes in mm the diameter of the "objective lens," usually the wider lens. My binoculars are 10X40 by Nikon. The first binoculars I owned were 7X35.

When you buy binoculars, always remember this one thing, and don't listen to anyone who tells you differently! The price you pay for your first binoculars is directly proportionate to how much abuse they will take. You will not see more birds or see them relatively better if you spend $500 or $50. But if you drop or bump the $50 binoculars, you may as well throw them away, because, after the bump, you'll be seeing two of everything; they're wrecked. If you drop $500 binoculars, you should be able to pick them up and keep right on going. When you get into the $900-1200 range for binoculars (I've never been there), you get more light and a brighter image; there is a clear difference when you buy the optimum binocular. But for where we are and what we're talking about, $80 - $300 is the price range.

So now that you have your binoculars, keep them handy all the time. A whole new world is about to open up for you. I keep my binoculars at my feet on my car floor. That way, I always know where they are and they're easy to grab if I stop to look at a bird. One piece of good advice is to throw those lens covers away as soon as you get new binoculars. You don't need them. If you have a pair that covers the eyepieces and are attached to the strap so you can put them down over the eyepieces in the rain, fine. Otherwise you'll be so ticked off when the peregrine flies by at warp 9 and you look up to see blackness because you forgot to take the caps off. You think I'm kidding? I'm not. Get rid of 'em.

Remember — binoculars only work when you put them up to your eyes! If you want to go on a nice walk in the country and you just let those binoculars hang around your neck, you're not birding, you're walking. No matter where you are, use your binoculars! Put them up to your eyes all the time; check out everything! You don't need to see a bird before you put the binoculars up to your eyes. It's good to look through binoculars, and when other people see you doing it and they'll use theirs too!

You're definitely going to start seeing things, no question about it. You'll find yourself saying things like "Are you seeing that bird going left, out over the big pines?" "Ya, what is it?" You'll find a lot of birds by scanning the horizon, the water surface, the tidal flats, and even the city skyline. Look out over the fields and meadows, even up into the sky. Someday you'll be standing at a beautiful spot somewhere in the wilderness and you'll scan the sky and see an eagle! You think I'm kidding? I'm not. Use your binoculars!

Using the naked eye you may see a bird fly into a tree or thicket, or perhaps spot one sitting perfectly still in the top of a tree for a long time (an ideal but infrequent opportunity), but then have a hard time finding it in your binoculars! This is very common for the beginner. Remember that everything is magnified several times, so things look very unnatural to your eyes. They're not used to focusing on magnified objects. So when you're trying to locate a bird in a tree or thicket, remember these key points:

1. Pre-focus your binoculars. As you stand in the area where birds may be active in front of you or nearby, get focused on the general area where the birds are. Then, when you spot the bird, you'll be ready to note key field marks. Again, don't sweat it if the bird gets away, there will be plenty more! Remember if you pre-focus your binoculars on nearby habitat, it's easier to make a quick, fine focus on the bird, rather than to watch in frustration as the bird moves off while you frantically fiddle with the focus ring.

2. Be patient. If you still can only see the bird or birds in the tree with your naked eye but can't pinpoint the location while looking through the binoculars, don't worry; this is a common thing. Orient yourself using a strong visual feature, like the trunk of a tree, a fork in the tree, or a particular branch. Look at the bird with your naked eye, find a nearby feature in the tree that's big enough or distinctive enough that you can find it with your binoculars, then orient left, right, up or down to locate the bird. You're already pre-focused on the tree so the bird is suddenly right there!

Getting Started

As a beginner, you may choose to go bird watching with an organized group. The local Audubon Society, bird club, or nature center near your home probably has bird walks throughout the year. Go along on one of these and just listen and learn. You'll find that there are so many species or kinds of birds that it may seem overwhelming at first, but believe me, once you get out a few times you quickly recognize the common birds and you'll find yourself looking for new species. Keep a list of the species you've seen and before you know it, a year will have gone by and you'll be feeling quite good about yourself. But wait, let's not get ahead of ourselves. Go on a few walks and keep the binoculars handy, look at everything! I mean it; don't let any bird get away. Most important, don't worry if you can't identify it. You don't have to know what you're looking at all the time. Enjoy the beauty of birds, and as you go, you'll pick things up here and there.

Identification

Okay, now we know what we have to do, so let's get down to the nitty gritty. How do I know what I'm looking at? How do I identify a bird once I see it? Remember, though, birding is not a pressure hobby and the more you do it, the better you will get at it. See what you can and be satisfied, at least at first. Don't sweat the identification. If you are with an experienced birder or group leader, and s/he says, "look at this," then look at it.

When you get down to the fun of actually identifying the bird, the following key points will help you nail it, as well as help you to develop into a complete and confident birder. Each time you go out, you'll gain confidence. Certain key points, names, sounds, and behaviors will become logged into your mind to be referred to automatically, time after time, year after year. Eventually, each bird you observe is subconsciously scrutinized so that the factors narrow down the possibilities. Interestingly, you often identify a bird not so much by what it is, but what it isn't! That may sound strange, but soon you'll understand and agree. Watch.

1. Judge the size. This is really the first and most important feature of a bird. Is the bird sparrow, robin, or crow-sized, smaller or larger?

Some birds are tiny, chickadee-sized or smaller. These include kinglets and some warblers, which are tiny little sprites and usually move quickly along through the branches. If you begin your birding experience in May, when warblers, vireos, and other high-energy songbirds are moving through, you'll find yourself spinning in circles. The brightly colored warblers, no matter how brilliant they are, blend perfectly with the sun-spattered woodland of buds, new leaves, and tree flowers. Lots of fun! So remember, a small bird in the field would be considered sparrow-sized by definition.

Robin-sized birds are average sized, ranging from cardinals to jays. Blackbirds, grosbeaks, orioles, many shorebirds and terns, fit into this average sized category. Many of these are among the commonest birds we know and are often "big" enough to get a pretty good look at. Consider though a flock of blackbirds, where there may be 4, 5, or 6 species hanging out together. More fun!

Crows, many ducks, hawks, and gulls fit into the crow-sized category and should be the easiest to identify. Now, I may have spoken too quickly here, because a whole chapter could be written on the identification of gulls alone, not so much because of the diversity of species, but by the somewhat confusing plumage patterns, leg color and bill pattern that tends to challenge even the most experienced birders. But, of course, that's why you have the binoculars up to your eyes, to have fun and try to figure them out!

Of course many birds are bigger still. Herons, eagles, vultures, some gulls, and pelicans (only 2 to choose from, brown or white) are all big birds.

When you first see a bird, put it into a size category, that will eliminate a lot of possibilities. Make your own judgment on size, sparrow, robin or crow, and go from there.

2. Determine what type of bird it is— what family. Is the bird you're watching a perching bird like a crow, robin, or other songbird? Is it a heron with a long pointed beak, long neck and legs? Is the bird a duck or other duck-like swimming bird? It could be a grebe or a loon. Does it look like a soaring hawk, or is it at the beach or on the tidal flats like a sandpiper or plover?

Sort the birds out and narrow down the possibilities. Each family of birds has distinctive characteristics. When you're just starting out, it can be a challenge just to decide what type of bird it is, let alone the exact species. Cormorant or loon? There's a good one for you.

Which features are distinctive?

What do you notice about the overall shape and form of the bird?

Eyestripe
Crown
Lores
Nape
Forehead
Back
Cheek
Wing Bars
Throat
Secondaries
Chest
Rump
Side
Tail
Belly
Primaries
Undertail Coverts
Flanks

The beak and head. Some bills will tell you right away what species it is, like the bill of an oystercatcher or Whimbrel. When combined with another observations, like its habitat, this can help you determine the type of bird. You will be best served by getting to know all about the bird to help you figure out who it is.

It gets a little more complicated when you try to separate a vireo from a warbler by the bill shape, but it's do-able. By the time you get to that point, you'll be noticing lots of things that you don't see now. So look at the bill. Better yet, look at the whole head. Several features of the head will help you identify a bird to species. Bill shape, overall head shape, eye size, eye color, and general plumage or color pattern. Does the bird have an eye stripe? An eye ring? All these factors, separate or combined, will help in identifying a bird.

5. Think about what the bird is doing.

Learning bird behavior can certainly help the novice or the experienced birdwatcher gain insight as to the identification of a bird. There's even the phenomena called "jizz" which among birders is the "feeling' that a bird was what it was. "I thought it was a peregrine falcon but it was out of sight before I got a good look at it. But it had a certain jizz, I'm sure it was a peregrine." When you just know that's what it was, even if you really didn't get a good look, there was that jizz.

If the bird is in flight, is it hovering in one spot above the water or land? Does the bird fly singly like a crow or jay, or do you see a flock of birds, also like crows, but more typically like blackbirds or finches. Is it a great flock or a well-designed V? Is the flight direct or is it undulating? When over water, do the birds fly close to the water or high above it? Is the bird soaring in large circles?

When sitting on the water does the bird occasionally dive? Does it "tip up" to feed like the dabbling ducks? Remember that sandpipers peck and feed as they walk, while a plover runs, stops and pecks, then runs again.

When watching warblers, note the "use of the tree" by the bird. Does it walk and clamor over the bare branches like a Black and White Warbler? Does it hover at the tips of twigs and pick insects from the leaves or needles like a Black-throated Green Warbler? Or is it on the ground or low in the undergrowth like a Palm Warbler?

Most importantly of all remember what you see. Seeing knows! Once you see a Prairie Warbler throw back its head, point its bill to the sky, and sing that loud song, rising up the scale, you will never forget the bird or the song!

Awareness of your surroundings, your ability to see and understand what surrounds you in nature, and your caring for not only the birds but all of the realms of nature of which you have now become part, make you a better birdwatcher.

Thank you for reading this, I hope it has excited you and given you the confidence to go out and identify birds.

Use a field guide after you have looked at the bird or birds, look at the field guide when you take a break from birding. Don't get frustrated!

Be patient!
Remember to use your binoculars!
Everywhere, all the time!
HAVE FUN!

Accounts of
INDIVIDUALSPECIES

Loons
& Grebes

On Cape Cod, we see two species of loons and three species of grebes. The Common Loon, Horned Grebe, and Pied-billed Grebe are seen easily in certain habitats. The Red-necked Grebe and Red-throated Loon are less common and appear in habitats similar to those of the Common Loon and Horned Grebe, in the open waters of Cape Cod Bay, Nantucket Sound, and the Atlantic Ocean.

Loons and grebes differ from ducks in their plumage pattern, shape and form. Primarily seen in non-breeding plumage, loons and grebes are dark birds with white chins, cheeks, and throats. Their beaks are more pointed than those of ducks. The exception is the Pied-billed Grebe, a freshwater or saltmarsh creek grebe that is small, stocky, and brown overall in appearance. I think it rather looks like a small, brown, swimming chicken.

Observe persistently, for loons and grebes are deep divers and may remain submerged for up to a minute or more.

{ Common Loon | BREEDING

WINTER | Common Loon}

28-36″
(Sept.- May)

Common Loon

Found on large bodies of water, mostly open ocean. A large, duck-like bird with a dagger-like bill. Seen most often in non-breeding plumage, although when coming from or, more likely, going to the breeding grounds in late summer and late spring, we may observe the dark neck and head and more sharply defined breeding plumage. Most often, Common Loons appear dark, sometimes speckled, on the back, with a white cheek, throat, and breast. They are usually solitary, but may appear in twos and threes, especially during migration. When the bird is swimming, it appears long-bodied.

Red-throated Loon

25"
(Oct.- May)

    Seen in non-breeding plumage on the open ocean, mostly along the outer beach from Provincetown to Chatham, and in Cape Cod Bay. This slender loon is often seen swimming in or just beyond the breaking waves on the outer beaches. Smaller and more petite in appearance than the Common Loon, with the same basic color pattern, but paler gray above. Bill appears to angle slightly upward and is thinner than Common Loon's. This is a grayer, smaller loon with a thin, upturned bill.

12-15″
(Sept.-May)

Horned Grebe

Seen most often on the open ocean, including Nantucket Sound, in non-breeding plumage. Dark gray, almost blackish above, with white cheeks and throat. Small, dark, pointed bill. As with all the loons and grebes, the Horned Grebe occurs singly or in small groups.

Pied-billed Grebe

13"
(spring & fall)

Found on freshwater ponds and lakes. A small brown bird with pointed chicken-like bill. Birds in breeding plumage have a dark ring on bill and a black throat. When seen swimming on freshwater ponds, the Pied-billed Grebe appears small, brown and round.

Shearwaters & Storm-Petrels

These birds are true seabirds and are seen primarily from boats. It's possible to observe shearwaters and petrels from some outer beaches during the summer months, but a spotting scope is necessary to make a positive identification, as they are typically off shore. These oceanic species may also be observed from certain shorelines or beach locations during northeasterly gales. On whale watches, two species of shearwater, the Great and Sooty, are commonly seen. A third species, the Manx, is uncommon but easily identifiable by its small size, and a fourth, the Cory's, is rare but has been observed regularly since 2009.

Storm-petrels are very small (smaller than a robin) and appear all black with a white rump. A relative of the shearwater, the Northern Fulmar is rare, but may be seen in the early spring or fall. Shearwaters, unlike gulls, soar close to the water's surface on narrow, stiff wings, and often rise in soaring circles off of the surface of large swells. Shearwaters and storm-petrels will follow boats if chum or food scraps are thrown overboard. Remember that the Sooty and Great Shearwater, as well as the Wilson's Storm-petrel, are southern hemisphere nesters, and appear in our North Atlantic Ocean waters as their wintering grounds, having flown "north" across the equator from the austral winter to the northern hemisphere summer.

Great Shearwater

19"
(May-Oct.)

A bird of the open seas and offshore waters. Observed near shore when blown in by nor'easters, storms with northeast winds. Dark brown above, pale underneath with a white rump patch. Look for a dark brown cap and a pale collar around the neck.

17"
(May-Oct.)

Sooty Shearwater

Frequently seen on summer whale watches. Any all-dark, chocolate brown shearwater is the Sooty Shearwater. Quite unmistakable.

The underwings, called the wing linings, (almost silvery) appear paler than the rest of the plumage.

Wilson's Storm-Petrel

7"
(May-Oct.)

Rarely observed except at sea, it is considered the most numerous seabird. A wandering, open ocean species. Cardinal-sized. All black with white rump; faint, whitish diagonal bar across each wing. This storm-petrel often follows boats and patters over the surface with legs dangling. Wilson's Storm-petrels that you see flying off the coast of New England in July and August may very well be nesting in a burrow, amongst penguins, in the Antarctic while you're celebrating New Year's day.

Gannets

38"
(Oct.-May)

Northern Gannet

A very large white seabird with black wing-tips. Appears pointed on four sides: at each wing, the beak, and the tail. Dives beak-first from high above the water. Often seen in large numbers. This large seabird is easy to identify because of large size. Seen from the shore in Cape Cod Bay and from Provincetown to Chatham during fall, winter and spring. Immature birds are the same size and overall shape as adults and may be either solid brown or blotchy brown and white in plumage pattern depending on their age. Northern Gannets reach maturity, their pure white and black plumage, in five years.

Cormorants

Cormorants are tall, upright standing, black birds, which occur singly or in groups. Unlike most other birds, they lack the oil gland that is used to oil their feathers to waterproof them. Cormorants may therefore become water-soaked when they dive. Hence, the familiar pose of cormorants standing with wings open, drying in the sun, is typical. Two species of cormorants occur on Cape Cod. One species is observed primarily in summer, the other in winter. There is little seasonal overlap.

Double-Crested Cormorant

33"
(April-Nov.)

Seen over the entire Cape, often standing on docks, jetties, boats, or pilings with wings spread. Double-crested Cormorants may be seen as fly-bys in summer, spring, and fall, or flying overhead in flocks. Larger than a gull, all-black with orange throat patch. Immatures are brown with white throat and breast. Always look for the orange throat patch, actually a gular pouch. Cormorants appear to tilt head upward when swimming. This is the black, upright standing bird of summer.

37"
(Oct.-April)

Great Cormorant

This large cormorant is the winter replacement of the Double-crested Cormorant. Shape and habits are similar. Large, an all-black bird with a small yellow face patch bordered by a patch of white. Both adults and immature Great Cormorants show a white flank patch when in flight. Immatures are dark brown with pale throat and whitish belly. This is a good bird to look for on the Provincetown breakwater in the fall and winter. Remember, a general rule of thumb is: Double-crested Cormorant occurs in summer; and Great Cormorant, in winter. There is little seasonal overlap but always worth a second look.

Herons & Egrets

Herons are long-legged, mostly long-necked, wading birds of the fresh and saltwater shorelines and marshes. The herons and egrets most often seen on Cape Cod are the Snowy Egret, Great Egret, Great Blue Heron, Black-crowned Night Heron, and Green Heron. The American Bittern is rare, The Yellow-crowned Night Heron, Cattle Egret, Tricolored Heron, and Little Blue Heron are uncommon and rarely observed.

Snowy Egret

20-27"
(April-Oct.)

This is the small white egret is seen in summer along marsh edges and shorelines. All-white with black beak, black legs, and yellow feet. This is typically the small white egret of salt marshes and creek edges.

42-52"
(August-May)

Great Blue Heron

Like most herons, this heron feeds alone, but roosts in groups. Tall (3-4 feet), bluish gray, with a pale face and yellowish beak. This is the big gray heron of fall and winter. In flight, legs extend beyond body. This heron does not nest on the Cape, but there are nesting colonies in eastern Massachusetts.

Black-crowned Night Heron

23-28"
(year round, more common May-Oct.)

Often seen roosting in trees. Boldly patterned, gray, black and white. Black cap, back, and bill. Gray neck and wings. White throat, breast and belly. Immatures are brown and streaked. Over ninety-nine percent of brown streaked herons are immature Black-crowned Night Herons. Black-crowns fly overhead at dusk calling a throaty *kwok*.

16-22"
(May-Sept.)

Green Heron

Solitary, nests in trees. Small, crow-sized heron with yellow legs. This is a fresh water habitat heron and is most often found at pond edges, but may certainly occur along salt marsh creeks. Dark green with chestnut neck and face, yellow legs, and bill. Most often seen perched motionless at water's edge. Call is a sharp *"kyew."*

Swans & Geese

Mute Swan

60"
(year round)

An introduced species from Europe. Unmistakable, large and all-white, orange bill with a black knob at the base of bill. The only swan you are likely to see on Cape Cod. This large invasive species tears up bottom vegetation from ponds and may discourage the presence of native waterfowl species.

25-43"
(year round)

Canada Goose

Needs little description. Common and widespread. Black head and neck, with a white bar on the chin and cheek. Brownish gray on back with pale underparts. Shows white band on rump in flight. Often seen flying noisily overhead or in large flocks, grazing in fields and marshes. Canada Geese have become abundant because of all of the green grassy fields and golf course we have built for them as feeding areas.

Brant

22-26"
(Oct.-May)

A small, dark saltwater goose. Black head, neck, and breast. Dark brown back with white visible on the tail and a faint white mark on the sides of the upper neck. This small arctic goose is very common swimming or roosting along the shores of Cape Cod Bay in winter.

Ducks

Ducks are grouped by behavioral characteristics related to feeding habits. Dabbling ducks tip up to feed, with their tail up and head submerged, feeding on submerged vegetation in shallow water. Dabblers spring from the surface to become airborne.

Diving ducks use large, webbed feet for swimming underwater, and use short, pointed wings for steering as they chase fish and invertebrates or feed on bottom plants. Diving ducks must run across the water's surface and flap to become airborne.

Diving ducks occur on both freshwater ponds and saltwater bays and may be observed in the company of dabbling ducks. Some females are difficult to identify from a distance, but males are easy to sort out with the help of a few simple markings.

Some diving ducks, the scoters, Common Eider, Common Goldeneye, and Bufflehead, are most often associated with saltwater bays and open ocean. A genus, or subgroup, of diving ducks, scoters are represented by three different species. All three scoters can be seen in Cape Cod Bay, off the Outer Cape, and in Nantucket Sound, often in large rafts.

An enjoyable winter's day of birding can be achieved by driving from pond to lake to bay to ocean, observing and identifying the great diversity of beautifully colored ducks and other waterfowl found in the cape's waters.

Dabbling Ducks

Mallard

20-28"
(year round)

The very common, green-headed duck. Male has white neck ring and rusty breast. Speculum is blue with white edges. Female is light brown with dusky orange bill.

Mallards can be found in most ponds on the Cape.

21-25"
(year round)

American Black Duck

In winter, the Black Duck is found in salt marshes and brackish water along the shore, often in flocks. Both sexes are dark brown with paler brown head. Mustard yellow bill. Speculum is purple with no white edges.

Northern Pintail

26-30"
(year round,
most often seen
Sept.-April)

A distinctive brown, white, and gray duck. Male has brown head with white slash extending up from brown neck. Back and sides are gray. Long pintail is black and acute. Female is mottled brown with black bill. Notice long neck in both sexes. Not widespread on the Cape. In winter, look at Hallets Mill Pond off Route 6A in Cummaquid, Barnstable.

18-23"
(year round,
most often seen
Sept.-April)

American Wigeon

Gray face, white forehead and crown, and green patch through the eye set this handsome duck apart from the others. Female head is plain gray. Both sexes have light, rusty brown breast and sides. Often seen in mixed flocks with other dabblers Look for this species, and others, at the mill pond, intersection of Rt. 149 and Rt. 28 in Marston's Mills. This bird also occasionally occurs at Great Pond, Eastham.

Green-winged Teal

14"
(year round,
most often seen
March-April and
Sept.-Nov.)

A very small duck. When a flock of dabblers is observed overhead, teal are half the size of the others. Male has chestnut head with green patch through eye. Female is small and brown with small bill and green speculum. Look in the eastern marshes and reservoir at the Harwich Conservation Area

15-16"
(April-Oct.,
uncommon)

Blue-winged Teal

Male has gray head with distinctive white crescent on face in front of eye. A very small duck. Female is brown overall and difficult to distinguish from Green-winged Teal. Both sexes have a relatively large bill and powder blue fore-wing patches. This small, beautiful duck may also be observed on the east side reservoir at the Harwich Conservation Area in March or April.

Wood Duck

18"
(year-round)

A distinctively beautiful, small to medium sized duck. Male Wood Ducks are unmistakable with a tufted green head with white facial markings, bright eye and rusty breast. Brightly colored overall. Female appears light or pale brown overall with a white eye patch.

Diving Ducks

15-18"
(Oct.-April)

Ring-Necked Duck

Black and gray. Black head, chest, and back; gray sides. Note vertical white slash between dark chest and gray sides. This field mark will signify the male ring-neck at a distance. Both sexes have a white ring on bill. Female is brown with faint white eye-ring. Found on lakes and ponds.

Greater Scaup

16-20"
(Oct.-April)

Similar to Ring-necked Duck, but no contrasting white slash on sides and no white ring on bill. This duck has a gray back, black breast, and white sides Female scaup have a white patch around the base of the bill on the face. Seen on bays and lakes. A few Lesser Scaup also occur here, but are scarce and very difficult to separate from the Greater Scaup. Lesser Scaup show less extensive white on the upper wing in flight, although most scaup are recorded as scaup sp. (species).

20-24″
(Nov.-March)

Canvasback

Uncommon, but often occur in large flocks when observed. A long-bodied duck with a sloping head and long bill. Chestnut head, black breast, black tail, pale gray sides and back. Female is similar to male but duller overall. Seen on freshwater ponds and in tidal rivers and bays. This species has occurred in past years at Walker's Pond, Brewster in late fall and winter.

Common Eider

23-27"
(Sept.-May;
a few present
all summer)

A large black-and-white duck with a distinctive pattern. Male has a tinge of yellow-green on the nape. Both sexes have a long, sloping forehead. Female is a rich, barred chestnut and dark brown. Often seen on the open ocean in rafts of hundreds or thousands, especially in Cape Cod Bay and off the outer Cape. Sub-adult males appear blotchy brown and white.

19"
(Oct.-April)

Black Scoter

A stocky, all-black duck with a distinctive orange knob at base of bill. Male shows no white anywhere.

Female is brown with pale cheeks and throat. Often seen off the outer beach in winter.

White-winged Scoter

21"
(Oct.-April)

Black overall with a white comma over the eye and small white patch (not always visible) on the side (wing). This is another big, impressive looking winter duck. In flight, it is the only all-black duck with large white patches on the rear of the wing. Female is brown overall; may also show the white patch on wing when swimming and has two pale patches on cheeks.

DUCKS
DIVING DUCKS

19"
(Oct.-April)

Surf Scoter

Black overall with a black, orange, and white bill. White patch on forehead and nape, thus its nickname "skunkhead." Female is similar to female White-winged Scoter, but has no wing patch. When in flight, this scoter shows the contrasting white patches on the head and nape very clearly to help in identification.

Common Goldeneye

18"
(Nov.-March)

Dark head with round white patch between eye and beak. White breast and sides. Dark back with white streaks on upper back. Female is grayish with brown head and a mostly black beak with a yellow tip. Most often observed on bays and large lakes. Pleasant Bay in Chatham and Orleans is one spot to find goldeneye, as well as Hallet's Mill Pond, Cummaquid, north of Rt. 6-A.

13-15"
(Nov.-April)

Bufflehead

A very small, chunky, black-and-white duck. Very common and widespread on both fresh and saltwater. Male has a big white patch on glossy, black head. Back is black; breast and sides, white. Female is dark brown with a white patch on cheek behind the eye. One of the commonest winter ducks.

Mergansers

Mergansers are fast-flying, fish-eating ducks. Beaks are thin and have serrated upper and lower mandibles. The Red-breasted Merganser is one of the most common saltwater ducks. Often hundreds can be seen in a day.

Red-breasted Merganser

20-26"
(Oct.-May)

Observed most often on saltwater in two plumages. Adult males show dark green head and shaggy crest, white neck ring, gray, black, and white sides. Females and immatures are brownish overall, with a rusty brown crest, head, and neck. Notice long neck and white wing patches as this bird flies in small groups fast and low over the water.

22-26"
(Nov.-March)

Common Merganser

Found on lakes and ponds, this large, white-sided, green-headed bird has a bright red beak and no crest. Female is large and rusty brown overall and has a white patch on the throat. They are not always as common as their name implies, so a sighting of this large duck is a special event.

Hooded Merganser

16-19"
(Oct.-April)

Uncommon but regular and found in ponds or brackish water. Male has striking, rounded white crest, fringed by black; black neck and black-and-white breast. This bird's mohawk of black and white should help to identify it. Females are also crested, but rusty brown overall. Small, woodland ponds are a good habitat in which to look for "hoodies". At Nickerson State Park, Brewster, and Jemima Pond, Eastham, are good spots to find this, the smallest merganser.

Hawks, Ospreys, Eagles & Vultures

Raptors appear in good numbers on the Cape, both as migrants and nesters. Hawks are generally separated into three groups, which describe their overall shape and behavior.

Buteos are the soaring hawks, often observed circling overhead on broad wings, with tails fanned. Included in the Buteo group and common on the cape are the Broad-winged Hawk and most often observed, the Red-tailed Hawk.

Accipiters are the fast-flying, bird-eating woodland hawks. Accipiters have short, rounded wings and a long tail, which aid in maneuverability through woods and thickets. Typical flight consists of several flaps, then a glide, then flapping and gliding repeatedly. This flight pattern is easily observed during spring and fall migrations. Accipiters include the Sharp-shinned Hawk, Cooper's Hawk and the rarely occurring Goshawk.

Falcons are swift, powerful hawks, with pointed wings and a long tail. Falcons feed primarily on small birds. Our smallest falcon is the Kestrel, which hovers when hunting. Other falcons include the Merlin and Peregrine.

Turkey Vulture

26-32"
(March-Sept.)

Large, dark, soaring bird with two-toned, light-gray/dark-gray underwings. When soaring, Turkey Vultures hold their wings in a shallow V, and teeter or see-saw with the wind. Often seen soaring over highways. Turkey Vultures have become more common over the last few decades and are now seen regularly, often in numbers, as they soar and glide over the capes roadways and marshes.

13-15"
(Nov.-April)

Northern Harrier

(formerly called Marsh Hawk)

This long-winged, long-tailed hawk is often seen flying low over salt marshes and dunes. A white rump patch seals the identification of this fairly common hawk. The harrier holds its wings in a shallow V in flight. Most harriers observed are brown females and similar, tawny colored immatures; the gray males are less frequently observed.

Sharp-shinned Hawk

10-14"
(Sept.-May)

A small, blue jay-sized, bird-eating hawk. Long tail and short, rounded wings identify this, the only small hawk with unpointed wings. Most often seen in flight which characteristically consists of several flaps, then a glide. This is the small hawk that terrorizes bird feeders. Adults show steel blue-gray upper parts and rusty barred breast while immatures are streaked brown overall.

16"
(year round)

Cooper's Hawk

Coopers's Hawk now nests on Cape Cod and can be seen throughout the year. This bird eating hawk is similar in appearance to the Sharp-shinned Hawk, but bigger, almost crow-sized. Adults appear steel blueish-gray on the mantle with a rusty barred breast, while immatures are streaked brown overall. Sometimes appears to have a crested appearance as this fearless raptor seems always alert, and ready for action.

Broad-winged Hawk

14-19"
(April-Sept.)

Crow-sized, our only other common, broad-winged, fan-tailed, soaring hawk. Overhead, distinguished from the Red-tail Hawk by smaller size and wide, black-and-white bands on tail: look for these two field marks first. Immatures are brownish with narrower, paler tail bands. Often seen in numbers during spring migrations, particularly over the Outer Cape. The Broad-winged Hawk nests in the pine/oak woodlands of the cape.

19-25"
(year round)

Red-tailed Hawk

A large, soaring hawk. Broad wings; pale under-parts with a brown belly band, and fanned, red tail are obvious as the adult Red-tail soars overhead. Immatures are similar to adults but show a brown rather than "red" tail. Our commonest large hawk; often seen along the highway.

Osprey

21-25"
(March-Oct.)

A large, distinct, sharply contrasting dark-brown-and-white fish hawk. Often seen flying fairly high overhead. In flight, Ospreys show a distinctive crook, or bend, in the wings. Nesting platforms have contributed to a welcomed recovery of this species over the last few decades. Ospreys are now observed over virtually all of Cape Cod, often at the nest.

9-12"
(year round)

American Kestrel

Smallest North American falcon. Dove-sized. Long tail and pointed wings. Males are steel blue on upper wings; females have brown upper wings and back (mantle). A true wire bird, kestrels often perch on overhead wires along roadways and watch the ground below for mice and insects. Kestrels hover when hunting. This small falcon has become increasingly rare over the cape, if not its entire range. Look for Kestrels along the Morris Is. Dike in Chatham.

Bald Eagle

30 – 32"
(year round)

A very large, buteo-shaped raptor. This huge bird is most often seen in its immature plumage; dark overall with variable amounts of white or pale plumage on the underside and wing linings. Often seen soaring high overhead. We rarely see adult Bald Eagles, although with nesting birds just off-cape in southeastern Massachusetts, the possibility becomes more likely each year. Look for this eagle over the outer cape, especially Provincetown.

Pheasant, Grouse, & Bobwhite

Of the Ring-necked Pheasant, Ruffed Grouse, and Northern Bobwhite, only the Bobwhite needs to be mentioned in detail.

The **Ring-necked Pheasant** male is brilliantly colored, large, and long-tailed. Although duller than the male, the female is also large and long-tailed.

The **Ruffed Grouse** is brown, chunky, and crow-sized. Grouse may be seen streaking across the road or exploding into flight from the woodland floor in a roar of wings. Behavior and habitat of the Ruffed Grouse most often help to identify it.

Northern Bobwhite

8-11"
(year round)

A small chunky quail, often seen at feeders or crossing roads. Plumage is mottled reddish brown and white. Throat and the line through the eye are white. Our only small, quail-like bird. Often seen in groups (coveys) during fall and winter. Call is a ringing *bob-white*.

Rails

Three species of rails occur on Cape Cod. All are secretive and rarely seen. **Clapper Rails** are most often found in salt marshes. **Virginia Rails** and **Soras** are typically found in freshwater wetlands, especially cat-tail marshes. Rails are distinctively shaped, chicken-like birds, most often heard at dawn or dusk. Clapper and Virginia Rail calls consist of the repeated single notes *kak, kak, kak, kak, kak* and *kik-kik, kik-kik, kik-kik* respectively. Soras give a shrill whinny or sharp single whistle. The secretive nature of rails allows few observations by the casual bird-watcher.

Shorebirds
Oystercatchers, Plovers, & Sandpipers

Shorebirds represent the birds of the tidal flats and shore edges. Knowing the common plovers and sandpipers of Cape Cod is the key to learning about any uncommon and rare visitors. Of the fifteen species mentioned here, two-thirds may be observed in numbers ranging from single birds and small foraging groups to large flocks ranging from twenty to several hundred birds. These birds may be found in homogenous groups or in groups where several species are represented.

When sandpipers and plovers occur in mixed flocks, the two can be separated by their foraging behavior. Remember, plovers locate food visually-— they walk or run, stop, peck, run again, stop, and peck. Sandpipers feed quite differently. They use their tactile sense to locate food as they probe the substrate, feeding as they walk. Knowing these two types of behaviors will help to narrow your choices in identifying a shorebird.

17-21"
(April-Oct.)

American Oystercatcher

Unmistakable! A large black, brown, and white bird of the tidal flats. Large, bright orange bill; yellow eye with orange eye- ring; pink legs. Found on mussel flats and sand bars, particularly on South Beach and Morris Island, Chatham.

Semipalmated Plover

6-8"
(May & July-Oct.)

Our only small, ring-necked plover of the tidal flats that is dark brown above and white below.

One dark ring around the neck and a white forehead patch help to identify this small plover.

6-8"
(March-Sept.)

Piping Plover

Uncommon. These small sand-colored plovers nest and may be seen at several public beaches around the cape and the beaches of southeastern Massachusetts. Similar in size and appearance to Semipalmated Plover, but the Piping Plover is tan above, white below, with a single, dark, often incomplete, neck ring. Post breeding flocks of 10 or more Piping Plovers, adults and juveniles, may be observed on beaches prior to migration in late August or September.

Killdeer

9-11"
(March-Nov.)

Not easy to find on Cape Cod, this is the ring-necked plover of upland areas. Robin-sized with two dark neck rings. The killdeer is dark brown above, white below, and shows a rusty rump patch and tail in flight. Found in pastures, open sandy areas around bogs, and, interestingly, along the edges of mall and plaza parking lots, where they may nest on the expansive gravel covered roofs of large stores. Nests on gravelly soil. Loud call is *kill-dee, kill-dee* or *dee-dee-dee*.

10-14"
(year round;
most common April-
May &
July-Nov.)

Black-bellied Plover

The largest plover in North America. Males are unmistakable, with a black face, throat, breast, and belly. Young or molting males may be blotchy black. A bright white stripe extends from the crown, down the sides of the neck, to the sides of the breast. Back is mottled black and white. Females, juveniles, and winter males look like a completely different bird: mottled grayish brown above and whitish below. Often seen in large flocks in high marshes during fall. All plumages show black axillars, or armpits, and an all-white tail in flight. This is our largest and most common plover.

Greater Yellowlegs

14"
(April-May
and July-Nov.)

Medium to large-sized sandpiper with bright yellow legs. Blotchy, streaked, grayish brown and white overall. Often seen actively chasing small fish in shallow water. Call is a loud rapid three- or four-note *tew tew tew*. When observing Greater Yellowlegs, look among them for the smaller, thinner billed Lesser Yellowlegs. This smaller cousin is less frequently observed, but should always be considered as a possible sighting.

14-17"
(April-Sept.)

Willet

One of our largest sandpipers. Willets are grayish brown overall, with grayish or finely barred breast and pale belly. Legs and beak are gray. A fairly large, plain, nondescript sandpiper when at rest, but in flight the Willet shows large, white wing patches. This bird nests on the Cape in salt marshes and is very noisy from June to August. Call is repeated *wi-wi-llet, wi-wi-llet, wi-wi-llet*. Willets nest primarily in beach grass along salt marsh edged all along the cape and may be heard during the summer before they are seen.

Whimbrel

15-19"
(July-Sept.)

Large and brown overall. Pale brown with streaks below and a striped crown of light and dark brown which shows a dark line through the eye. Most notable is the very long, de-curved bill. Found in salt marshes where it feeds on fiddler crabs.

8-10"
(May & July-Sept.)

Ruddy Turnstone

The calico cat of the bird world. Unmistakable; rich chestnut, black, and white with orange legs. Flips stone, shells and vegetation with its bill in search of food on sand and tidal flats. Hence the name Turnstone. If you've never observed a Ruddy Turnstone, your first sighting will be a pleasant surprise!

Red Knot

10-11"
(July-Sept.)

A medium-sized, chunky sandpiper with a relatively short bill and legs. May be observed in two distinct plumages. Fall and winter birds are a nondescript grayish and white; breeding birds show a robin-red breast and belly. Birds in either plumage may appear together on tidal flats. Remember, its short beak distinguishes the Red Knot from the Short-billed Dowitcher, which has similar rusty plumage, but a very long beak.

7-8"
(April-Nov., but may winter over)

Sanderling

Small, pale gray sandpiper. Some appear on the Cape in breeding plumage, which is brick red on head, breast, and back. Belly is white. This is the bird that runs ahead of breaking waves as you walk along the outer beach. We see mostly the pearl gray, non-breeding plumage during the fall and winter months..

Semipalmated Sandpiper

5-7"
(May and
July-Sept.)

Small, very numerous sandpiper. Most often in large flocks on the tidal flats. Compare with tiny Least Sandpiper, which prefers muddy tidal creeks and salt marshes. Semipalmated is the small, black-legged, dark billed sandpiper of tidal flats. Somewhat nondescript; grayish brown above with pale breast and belly. Two small sandpipers are most frequently observed on the flats during late summer and fall; the Semipalmated Sandpiper and the Least Sandpiper. Separate the two quickly by comparing the tiny, rusty plumaged Least Sandpiper, which has yellowish legs, to the slightly larger, brownish Semipalmated Sandpiper which has black legs.

5-7"
(April-May
& July-Sept.)

Least Sandpiper

Our smallest shorebird. Has yellowish legs and prefers salt marshes and muddy tidal creeks. Rusty brown on back and pale below. Any small sandpiper that flushes from a salt marsh is almost certainly a Least Sandpiper. Call is *breep, breep, breep*.

Dunlin

8-9"
(April-May
& Sept-Nov.;
winters over)

This is a smallish, long-billed sandpiper that occurs in two plumages. In spring, the Dunlin shows a rusty back with a rectangular, black belly smudge. Seen mostly in late fall in plain plumage of grayish brown and pale gray. Our latest arriving fall shorebird. Note relatively long bill on this small, grayish brown bird.

10-12"
(July-Sept.)

Short-billed Dowitcher

Dowitchers are medium-sized and chunky. Appears brownish red overall; easiest field mark is its long, straight bill. Also shows a pale eye stripe and, in flight, a white stripe up the middle of back. Dowitchers are often observed in large flocks.

Gulls & Terns

Gulls and terns are closely related species, gray above and pure white below, except the Great Black-backed Gull, which is black above. These are birds of the lakes and ponds, seashore and open ocean, often observed foraging along beaches. Terns tend to be smaller and appear more streamlined than gulls. Terns can be separated from gulls by their small size and black cap.

Great Black-backed Gull

28-31"
(year round)

Our largest gull needs little description. White head, breast, and belly; black back and wings. Takes four years to acquire adult plumage.

Immatures appear mottled brown overall, with varying degrees of black on back, depending on age.

23-26"
(year round)

Herring Gull

The common "sea gull" with white head, breast, and belly, and pale gray back and wings. Yellow bill with red spot near tip; pink legs. Takes four years to acquire adult plumage. Immatures appear mottled brown overall, with varying degrees of gray on back, depending on age.

Ring-billed Gull

19"
(year round)

A small version of the Herring Gull, with two main differences. Adults have yellow bill with black ring near tip and yellow legs, rather than pink. Ring-bills often flock in school yards, open fields, and parking lots. They nest around the Great Lakes and winter here, but some non-breeders are here in summer. Takes three years to mature. Immatures appear mottled brown overall, with varying degrees of gray on back, depending on age.

16-17"
(April-Oct.)

Laughing Gull

Our only common gull with a black head. Takes three years to mature. Immatures appear as a small, dusky grayish brown gull. Call is a loud *hah-hah-hah-haaaah*, with variations. They nest on Monomoy Island, Chatham.

Black-legged Kittiwake

17"
(Sept.-April)

A small, gray-and-white winter gull of the open sea. Occasionally seen in huge numbers off the Outer Cape in winter. Two good field marks are its small, unmarked yellow bill, and its all-black wing tips (they look as if they have been dipped in ink). Winter juveniles have a black bill and a distinct, black W pattern across the wings that contrasts with a white wedge on rear of wings.

13-16"
(May-Oct.)

Common Tern

Most large terns seen in summer along the shores of Cape Cod are Common Terns. Gray above, white below; black cap, orange bill with a black tip, and a deeply forked tail. Call is a *kee-eer* or *kip-kip-kip*. Look for Common Terns flying and foraging for small fish along the shore or in large flocks over schools of bait fish.

Roseate Tern

14-17"
(May-Sept.)

Uncommon but may be seen among flocks of Common Terns. Roseate Terns are silvery white with black bill and long, white, flowing tail feathers. Listen for its call, *chi-vik, chi-vik*. This federally endangered species is rarely seen away from the breeding grounds. Roseates nest on Bird Island, Marion and Ram Island Mattapoisett. Some may breed on Monomoy Is., Chatham. These are protected areas and should not be approached, although these beautiful silvery terns may be observed adjacent to these areas as they forage for food.

9"
(May-Aug.)

Least Tern

Our smallest tern. Gray above, white below, with a black cap and a yellow beak. Forehead is white. This delicate little tern is widespread, and may be seen diving for fish in fresh as well as salt water. Most often seen along the outer beaches and along beaches and shorelines.

Doves & Pigeons

We have one dove and one pigeon on Cape Cod. Both are very common, but live very different lives.

Rock Dove

13"
(year round)

The basic pigeon. Typically gray and iridescent, but hybrids range from multicolored gray, white, and black to all-white or all-brown. Nests under highway bridges, on buildings, or church steeples.

| 12"
(year round) | **Mourning Dove** |

A medium-sized, brownish gray dove with a long, pointed tail. Some iridescence and pinkish buff are visible on the neck. Head appears relatively small. Often seen on wires and in areas with bird feeders. Inhabits open areas and fields.

Owls

There are two common owls on Cape Cod and they are both very widespread. The Great Horned Owl is big and eats whatever it wants. The Eastern Screech-Owl is small and lives in hollow trees. A third species, the Saw-whet Owl, is rarely seen, secretive, and heard mostly in coniferous woodlands. The Saw-Whet call is a long series of *toots,* repeated over and over.

18-25"
(year round)

Great Horned Owl

More often heard than seen. A very large owl with "ear" tufts and big, yellow eyes. Nests in large pines. Call of repeated, deep, loud hoots is heard most often during winter.

Eastern Screech-Owl

7-10"
(year round)

A small gray or reddish-brown owl with ear (feather) tufts. Screech Owls inhabit any area with large deciduous trees, particularly near water. Screech Owls may call anytime during evening hours, beginning just after dark and usually ending before dawn. Call is a soft, quavering trill or low, monotone, warbling whistle.

8"
(year round)

Northern Saw-whet Owl

This tiny owl is most often heard and rarely seen. Listen at night for its repetitious *toot, toot, toot, toot, toot, toot*, repeated several times, most often in conifers, Nickerson State Park, Brewster, and the White Cedar Swamp at the Marconi site, Wellfleet, are places to listen for this secretive little owl, especially in winter and spring.

Swifts

Chimney Swift

5-6"
(May-August)

The Chimney Swift is only seen in flight and can be identified by its call alone—a constant twittering overhead, especially at dusk during spring and especially summer. A small, dark "cigar with wings." Long wings and rapid wing beats identify this, our only swift.

Hummingbirds

3.75"
(May – Sept.)

Ruby-throated Hummingbird

This tiny hummingbird, our only resident hummer, is frequently observed in flower gardens as it sips nectar from a variety of flowers, lilies, phlox, jewelweed, and many others. The male is unmistakable with a ruby red throat, dark green back, pale green sides and a pale breast. The upper breast and neck ring are white. Females are green above and dull green below with a white throat. This is the hummingbird of Cape Cod and may be seen zipping by on any day afield

Kingfishers

Belted Kingfisher

13"
(year round)

A medium-sized, crested bird. Solitary, often perches on overhead wires or pilings. Richly blue head, breast band, back, and wings; white breast and neck ring. Female has a second rusty band across belly. This species exhibits sexual dimorphism, as the female is the more brightly plumaged of the pair. Feeds by hovering over a body of water and diving for live fish. Found near ponds, bays, and estuaries. Our only kingfisher.

Woodpeckers

We have four common woodpeckers on Cape Cod: two look very similar, but are different sizes, the third is a woodpecker that feeds mostly on the ground, and the fourth, the Red-bellied Woodpecker, is a new arrival to our woodlands.

9-10"
(year round)

Red-bellied Woodpecker

This handsome woodpecker is larger than the Hairy Woodpecker and shows a barred black and white back and wings with a bright red nape and cap. Juvenile birds and females show less red on the crown. This handsome woodpecker comes readily to suet feeders and sunflower seeds.

Downy Woodpecker

6-7"
(year round)

The small, black-and-white woodpecker of the woodlands and suet feeders. Sparrow-sized. Male shows red on back of head. Note thin bill and black spots on white outer tail feathers.

9-10"
(year round)

Hairy Woodpecker

Less common than the Downy Woodpecker. Noticeably larger than Downy, but nearly identical. Heavier bill than Downy Woodpecker and all-white outer tail feathers. Associated with extensive woodlands.

Northern Flicker

12-14"
(year round)

Robin-sized, often found on the ground where it feeds on ants. White rump patch immediately signifies the flicker when observed in flight. Yellow under-wings, spotted breast and belly, and barred back all help in identification, but look for white rump patch. Male has red patch on the back of head and black mustache on face.

Flycatchers

Four species of flycatchers are commonly seen on Cape Cod and all four are nesting species. These are small to medium-sized birds. All are 6-9 inches in length and can be separated easily for identification. Flycatchers habitually sit on a dead or exposed branch, flit out after an insect, and return to the same perch. Each of Cape Cod's common flycatchers has a distinct field mark that should help to identify it quickly, and the habitat of each one will also help identify it.

6-7"
(March-Oct.)

Eastern Phoebe

A bird that is almost always found near water. Olive brown above with whitish (yellowish in immatures) underparts; no wing bars. Song is a buzzy *fee-bee*. Look for tail movement up and down when it is perched. Nests under shack or garage eaves and under bridges near streams.

Great Crested Flycatcher

8-9"
(May-Sept.)

A bird of the oak woodlands; easier to hear than see. Dark olive above, white throat, yellow breast and belly. Appears slightly crested.

In flight, shows reddish flash in wings and tail. Listen for loud *wheep, wheep* call in tree tops.

8"
(May-Sept.)

Eastern Kingbird

Distinctly black above and pure white below. White band across end of tail. Often noisily twittering near pond edges. Occurs, more than other flycatchers, in open areas.

Eastern Wood Pewee

6"
(May – Sept.)

This is a bird of the Pine/Oak woodlands and is often heard before, and often rather than seen. Its plaintive *pee-o-weee*, is often heard in the still summer woods while the small olive and pale yellowish/green bird blends with the foliage. Two white wing bars separate it from the Eastern Phoebe, which would not typically be found in the woods. This small flycatcher is almost always heard before it is seen.

Larks

Only one species of lark is found on Cape Cod and it occurs year round both as a nester and winter resident. Found readily on beaches and dune areas.

7-8"
(year round)

Horned Lark

A ground-dwelling bird of open areas. Sometimes shows distinct, black horns against a face and throat of yellow; black eye patch. Brown on back with black breast patch and pale underparts. Depending on their sex and age, Horned Larks can be brightly and distinctly patterned or nondescript and brown. Habitat is a good clue to identification. Savannah Sparrows share the same habitat, but are heavily streaked and smaller. Listen for the Horned Lark's twinkly, metallic song on beaches. Often runs over dunes.

Swallows

Six species of swallows occur on the Cape, but only two are widespread and common. These are the Tree Swallow and the Barn Swallow. The Northern Rough-winged Swallow is brown above and white below on breast and belly and nests in sandbanks and cliffs or under bridges. Bank Swallows are almost identical, but have a brown band across the pale chest. The Cliff Swallow and Purple Martin occur while on migration and are rarely observed, although there has been recent breeding success of Purple Martins in Mashpee, and this species may be seen locally during the spring and summer breeding season.

Tree Swallow

5-6"
(April-Oct., abundant in Sept. during fall migration)

Males are bright blue above, pure white below. Females are similar, but duller blue gray. The common swallow of nest boxes. Zigzags over open areas to catch insects in flight. Does not have a deeply forked tail like our other common swallow, the Barn Swallow. During September, Tree Swallows migrate by the thousands along the shores of Cape Cod, sometimes in seemingly endless flocks.

6-8″
(April-Sept.)

Barn Swallow

Dark, rich blue above, cinnamon buff below, with a reddish throat. Note the deeply forked tail. Zips through the air to catch insects on the wing. Makes a net on the barns, rafters, bridges; often nests in groups.

Jays & Crows

Neither jays nor crows need much description. We see one species of jay on Cape Cod. In recent years, the smaller Fish Crow has increased its range eastward, to the area along the Cape Cod Canal and may range even further eastward to the Mid- and Outer Cape. The Fish Crow is almost identical to the American Crow but smaller and with a higher pitched, *caa, caa,* rather than the typical raucous *caw, caw,* of its larger cousin. Crows and jays are loud, rowdy, and intelligent.

Blue Jay

11-13″
(year round)

A bright blue, crested jay with a black necklace on white underparts. Blue Jays inhabit oak woods and visit feeders regularly. This is an unmistakable species

17-21"
(year round)

American Crow

This is our roadside crow, larger than the Fish Crow and any other black bird we see on the Cape. All black, including legs and bill. Often seen in flocks, especially aggressive when harassing hawks or Great Horned Owls.

Chickadees & Titmice

Our familiarity with the Black-capped Chickadee is probably greater than with the Tufted Titmouse. However, both are very common and related to each other. Both titmice and chickadees occur at bird feeders and are at home in the Cape's oak woodlands. Often these tough little birds flock together in winter, when they actively move about in search of insect eggs and larvae.

Black-capped Chickadee

4-6"
(year round)

Very common and widespread. Small, gray above, buffy below with a black cap and bib. Call is a nasal *dee, dee, dee* or *chik-a-dee dee dee*, in spring, a clear, two-note whistle.

6″
(year round)

Tufted Titmouse

Our only small gray-and-white, crested bird. Gray above, white and creamy buff below. Beady eyes and black patch on forehead. Call is a three or four note whistle, often given from treetops. Gives a nasal buzz when excited or alarmed.

Nuthatches

Two species of nuthatches occur on Cape Cod. Both may occur regularly at feeding stations. Nuthatches habitually walk headfirst down tree trunks and over branches. The White-breasted Nuthatch is a bird of the deciduous woodlands while the Red-breasted Nuthatch prefers the conifers. In the mixed pine/oak woodlands of the cape, both may be seen by the careful observer.

White-breasted Nuthatch

5-6"
(year round)

White face, black cap, and grayish-blue back and wings. White breast and belly with reddish flanks help to identify this acrobat of the oak woods and bird feeders. Slightly larger than a chickadee. Female has the same pattern but is duller overall. Call is a nasal *ank, ank*.

4"
(year round)

Red-breasted Nuthatch

A bird of the pine woods; smaller than a chickadee. Rusty breast and belly, rich, blue gray back, black cap, and black line through the eye against a white face. Female has same pattern but is duller overall. Also climbs headfirst down tree trunks. Fairly uncommon; numbers fluctuate year to year. Comes to feeders and beef suet.

Kinglets & Gnatcatchers

These tiny woodland sprites are associated mainly with spring and fall warbler migrations. The Golden-crowned Kinglet winters on the Cape and although they are fairly hard to come by, careful observation of mixed flocks of chickadees and titmice may turn up the elusive Golden-crowned Kinglet.

Ruby-crowned Kinglet

4"
(April-May
and Sept.-Oct.)

Tiny, olive green above, whitish below. Never stands still, constantly fluttering wings. Often seen in numbers during spring migration. Look for two yellowish wing bars and a white eye-ring.

3-4″
(Oct.-April)

Golden-crowned Kinglet

Tiny, olive green above, whitish below, but most easily identified by bright yellow-orange crown patch and a white line through the eye against a dark face. Prefers evergreens; often observed along wood edges and shrubbery in winter.

Blue-gray Gnatcatcher

4″
(April-May)

This tiny version of a mockingbird is seen mainly during spring migration. An active, long-tailed, gray-and-white bird with white outer tail feathers and a white eye-ring. Gray above, white below, with a black tail. Call is a nasal *speee*.

Thrushes

6-7"
(year round)

Hermit Thrush

This woodland thrush shows a distinctly rust colored tail in all plumages. Often seen on or near the ground, notice the pale rusty brown plumage on the back and head, with a spotted breast and pale belly. Look for a white eye-ring as this thrush scratches and moves along the leaf litter on the woodland floor.

American Robin

9-11"
(March-Oct.,
but some may
occur year round)

Dark gray back, males have a black head, rusty red breast. Seen on lawns and in junipers and berry bushes, very widespread. Listen for a song at dawn and dusk *cheeri-o, cheeri-o, cheeri-up*. I've always thought this beautiful robust thrush should be called Black-headed Thrush.

7"
(year round)

Eastern Bluebird

Eastern Bluebirds are found in open areas; meadows, bogs, fields, golf courses. Male is a bright blue above with a rusty breast and white belly. This small thrush is often seen on wires or fences along the road. Females are similarly patterned, but less bright overall. Nest boxes have helped increase the number of breeding pairs on the cape.

Mimic Thrushes

Three species of mimic thrushes occur on Cape Cod. The first, the Brown Thrasher, is less widespread and more secretive. The other two, the Gray Catbird an the Northern Mockingbird, are very common. All three mimic thrushes are excellent songsters. All like shrubs and thickets and have noticeably long tails.

Brown Thrasher

11-12"
(April-Oct.)

Looks like a cross between a thrush and a mockingbird. Rich, reddish brown above and heavily spotted below, but with a long tail. Adult Brown Thrasher has yellow eyes. Brown Thrashers are often seen or heard, foraging in the leaves of the forest floor, often under dense branches.

9"
(May-Oct.)

Gray Catbird

Dark gray overall with black cap, black tail, and chestnut brown undertail coverts. If you have shrubs and thickets in your yard, catbirds probably nest there. Song is a bubbly, squeaky, gurgling cacophony of notes; also makes a catlike meow.

Northern Mockingbird

9-11"
(year round)

A long-tailed, gray-and-white bird with large, white wing patches and white outer tail feathers. Gray above, darker tail and wings, white below. An excellent mimic, it imitates everything—from other birds and animals to music. Prefers multiflora rose and other thickets. May sing all night long. Look for the bright yellow eye.

Starlings

The starling is an introduced species which has become abundant throughout all of the United States. They often out-rival native species for nesting cavities.

(year round)

European Starling

A glossy black, short-tailed, black bird with yellow beak. Appears speckled during fall and winter. Often seen on wires or in treetops. Series of calls is a cacophony of squeaks, twitters, and chirps. Starlings form huge flocks in salt marshes during late summer and fall.

Vireos

Vireos are often associated with warblers, especially during spring and fall migrations. But, their bills are short and stout compared to the needle pointed, tweezer-like bill of warblers. Only the Red-eyed Vireo is common on the Cape, although the Solitary Vireo, with its bluish head, white spectacles, and white wing bars, occurs during migration and should be identifiable during spring migration, especially in May.

Red-eyed Vireo

6″
(May-Sept.)

Drab olive green on the back, but with a gray cap and a white stripe above the eye bordered above and below with black. This vireo sings all day, all summer, from tree-tops in deciduous woods. Much more often heard than seen; usually three or four melodious phrases sounding somewhat robin-like.

Warblers

The very word warbler excites novice and expert birder alike. For many, spring warbler migration is the most exciting time of year. Although the fall plumage of warblers is known to be nondescript, some males may be in full or partial breeding plumage during fall migration. All nineteen species mentioned here are common in breeding plumage during spring migration.

Warblers are tiny (chickadee-sized or smaller), brightly colored, fast-moving insect eaters. Their identification can be made easier by following a few basic steps.

First, separate warblers by determining whether or not the species has wing bars. This will cut your choices by about fifty percent.

Second, look on the breast for streaking or a "necklace." This will limit your choices further.

Third, look at the colors and pattern on the face and head. All warblers are distinctly different.

Rather than seeing them as a confusing group, sort each bird out and identify your bird by what it isn't, using the three steps above.

Warblers with Wing Bars

Northern Parula

4-5"
(May-Sept.)

A tiny, short-tailed, blue, yellow, and white warbler. Blue back, yellow throat, white belly. Two white wing bars. Male shows reddish and black across breast. Notice olive green patch on the back. Key your observation on blue, yellow, and white color pattern. Only two regularly occurring warblers have blue backs. The other is the Black-throated Blue Warbler which is a sharp, contrasting blue, black, and white pattern. The Northern Parula nests in a few spots on Cape Cod.

5-6"
(Sept.-May)

Yellow-rumped Warbler

Our only wintering warbler. The winter plumage is nondescript, streaked, brownish gray above and whitish below. Bright yellow rump in all birds. Breeding plumage is bluish gray, black, yellow, and white. Yellow rump, crown, and side patches; black face; white throat; bluish gray on back. White below with black across the breast. This is one of the earliest spring migration species to arrive on the Cape. In winter, often found in flocks among bayberry thickets on outer beaches.

Black-throated Green Warbler

4-5"
(May and
August-Sept.)

Should be called black-throated yellow warbler since its face, which contrasts with the black throat and bib, appears more yellow than green. Olive green on back; dark wings with white wing bars and white belly. Key on this bird's yellow face and black throat. Often seen in the outermost twigs of oaks and pines. Song is *zee-zee-zee-zoo-zee.*

WARBLERS WITH WING BARS

5-6″
(April-Oct.)

Pine Warbler

A somewhat drab, yellowish treetop warbler. Pine Warblers nest in tall pitch pines throughout Cape Cod. We rarely see them in the dense canopy they occupy, but their monotone, yet musical, trill is heard often, especially in May and June. Dull yellow breast, white belly, and two white wing bars help to identify this warbler. When the backbone of winter has broken and we await the relative warming of late March and April, listen for the early song of the Pine Warbler coming from high in the Pitch Pines.

Prairie Warbler

5"
(May-Sept.)

The Prairie Warbler is a common nester of open scrub lands, beach and marsh edges, and overgrown meadows. Also look along power lines where vegetation is low. Easy to identify by its distinctive song—a series of *zee* notes with a rising inflection. Prairie Warbler is olive on the back with yellow eyebrow, yellow patch below the eye, and bright yellow throat, breast, and belly. Shows black line through the eye and through the cheek; black specks on sides of body. Key on the song and a distinctive black-and-yellow face.

5"
(May-Sept.)

Black-and-white Warbler

Streaked black and white on face, throat, back, breast, and sides. Only the belly is pure white. Clings nuthatch-like to tree trunks and branches. Often seen in abundance during May. Song is a series of high, thin *wee-see, wee-see, wee-see, wee-see, wee-see*. This is one of the early spring migrants

Magnolia Warbler

4-5"
(May and Sept.)

Black, yellow, and white. Look for black face, yellow throat, white eyebrow, and white wing patch. Also shows a yellow rump patch and white patches on tail. Breast is yellow, with black streaks; belly is yellow. Focus on the black, yellow, and white color pattern and the white patches on the tail.

Warblers with No Wing Bars

5″
(May-Sept.)

Yellow Warbler

A common nester throughout the Cape, especially near water. Yellow overall, yellow olive on back. A short-tailed, yellow warbler we see all summer long.

Male has red streaks on breast. Song is *sweet, sweet, sweet, sweeter than swee*t. Inhabits woodland edges and wet areas.

Palm Warbler

5″
(April-May;
Sept.-Oct.)

A ground-dwelling warbler that appears yellow with a rusty cap in spring. This is the first warbler species to arrive in the spring. In fall migration, drab olive overall with a yellow rump. This species wags or pumps its tail up and down constantly—a good identification clue. Palm Warbler is usually on or near the ground.

5"
(May-Sept.)

American Redstart

Male is an unmistakable, glossy black with orange patches in wings and tail. Female is similarly patterned but grayish and dull yellow. Often flashes tail and wings while chasing insects. Like all warblers, the redstart is a tiny, fast-moving bird.

Common Yellowthroat

5"
(May-Oct.)

Olive on the back; bright yellow throat, breast, and belly. The male's bandit-like mask helps to identify it immediately. Female is olive with bright yellow throat.

Yellowthroats nest and forage low in dense shrubbery. I can't ever remember looking up at a Common Yellowthroat!

6"
(May-Aug.)

Ovenbird

A small thrush-like warbler; lives on the ground and is more often heard than seen. Song is a loud, repetitive *teacher, teacher, teacher, teacher, teacher,* which starts softly and becomes steadily louder. Olive above with white eye-ring and chestnut orange cap. Pale below with brown streaking. The Ovenbird is a common woodland nester on the cape.

Other Spring Warblers

Other spring warblers that the casual birdwatcher may encounter are:

Chestnut-sided Warbler | 5"

Wing bars. Yellow cap; black line through eye; chestnut sides.

Cape May Warbler | 5"

White wing patch. Chestnut face patch bordered with yellow; yellow throat; breast and belly heavily streaked with black.

Black-throated Blue Warbler | 5-6"

White wing patch. Vivid blue back and wings; black face, throat, and sides; white belly.

5" | ## Blackburnian Warbler

White wing patch. Fiery orange face
with black eye patch; black back.

5" | ## Blackpoll Warbler

White wing bars. Like Black-and-white
Warbler except all white face and black cap.

5" | ## Wilson's Warbler

No wing bars. Easy to identify—bright
yellow underparts and face with black cap.
Olive yellow back and wings.

5-6" | ## Canada Warbler

No wing bars. A beautiful, gray-backed warbler
with a yellow throat, breast and belly.
Note black necklace and white eye-ring.

Cardinals

Northern Cardinal

7-9"
(year round)

Everybody's favorite. All-red bird with crest. Male has a black face patch; female is a duller gray-green overall.

Towhees

7-9"
(April-Oct.)

Eastern Towhee

Formerly called Rufous-sided Towhee. A secretive bird, whose call—*chew-wink* or *drink-your-teee*—is often heard before it is seen. Male is black on head, back, and throat; sides bright rufous; belly white. Female is brown on head, back, and throat. This is a bird of scrub-oak and pine woodlands,

Sparrows & Wrens

Small, chiefly brown-and-white, ground-dwelling birds. Several show yellowish or buffy ochre highlights in plumage, especially on the face. Like the warblers, most of these are distinctly different in plumage patterns and habitat preference. So, when identifying sparrows, look at the habitat. Observe the sparrow's behavior—you will find some sparrows can be identified almost on the basis of behavior alone. When you note the field marks, look first at the breast to see if it is plain or streaked.

Chipping Sparrow

5"
(April-Oct.)

Clearly identified plumage; a chestnut cap, white eye stripe with a black lower edge; clean, white throat, breast, and belly identify this small, long-tailed sparrow. Look for chippies around and under pitch pines.

4-6"
(April-Nov.;
small numbers
occur year round)

Savannah Sparrow

This is the small, streaked sparrow of the open grassy dunes and meadows. Most sparrows seen in dune grass are savannahs. The Savannah Sparrow is similar to the Song Sparrow but shows pale yellow on face and has a shorter tail.

Saltmarsh Sharp-tailed Sparrow

5-6"
(May-Oct.)

A small, salt marsh sparrow with buffy underparts, gray nape, ochre face, and short tail. This is the sparrow of the salt marsh. Virtually any sparrow in the wetter areas of the salt marsh, usually in the tall cord grass, is a sharp-tailed.

5-7"
(year round)

Song Sparrow

Our most common sparrow. Sings from bush tops. Heavily streaked breast with center spot and long, often rusty looking tail helps to identify this widespread sparrow. Song starts with two or three notes, and continues with a short melody.

White-throated Sparrow

6-7"
(Sept.-May)

A larger-than-average sparrow of winter months. Bright white throat, gray breast and belly. Light-and-dark-striped crown with a yellow spot between bill and eye help to identify this ground-dwelling, feeder bird. This beautiful sparrow may be seen in abundance during the early weeks of spring migration.

6″
(Oct.-April)

Dark-eyed Junco

This is our gray-and-white snowbird. Gray above; with a white belly and white outer tail feathers which flash when in flight. A ground-dwelling bird, common at bird feeders during the winter months.

Carolina Wren

5-6"
(year round)

This loud and active wren of yards and gardens is often heard singing its repeated *creerily-cheerily-cheerily-cheerily* above all other bird songs. Chestnut brown overall, bright on the back and paler below with a distinct white eye stripe and slightly curved bill. Often visits feeders for sunflower chunks and suet.

Blackbirds

Three species of blackbirds occur on the Cape. (The aforementioned Starling is not in the blackbird family.) All blackbirds flock, that is, gather and move in numbers and are fairly easy to separate and identify, although the females can be confusing to beginners.

7-10"
(March-Nov.)

Red-winged Blackbird

Our common marsh blackbird. Black overall with orange/red shoulder patches trimmed in yellow. The "song" of the arriving male Red-winged Blackbirds in mid to late February is the harbinger of spring. Females look like big, heavily streaked sparrows.

Common Grackle

11-14"
(March-Nov.)

This is the glossy, long-tailed blackbird. Iridescent purplish-green on head, neck, and breast. Yellow eyes. Often in large flocks with other blackbirds. Found in all habitats, especially in residential areas.

7"
(April-Oct.)

Brown-headed Cowbird

A small, unfamiliar, yet common and widespread blackbird. Male is glossy black overall, but has a chocolate brown head. Most often seen walking on lawns. Female is mostly gray brown overall and nondescript. Cowbirds are parasitic, that is, they lay eggs in other birds' nests and depend on these nesters to rear their young.

Orioles & Finches

Baltimore Oriole

7-8"
(May-Sept.)

Bright-orange-and-black with white wing bars. Black head and wings; orange breast and belly. Tail is black with orange outer edges.

Female is drab overall. Nests high in trees; sings rich, musical notes from treetops.

5-6"
(year round,
abundant)

House Finch

This is the bird that everyone mistakenly calls Purple Finch. It is not the Purple Finch, which has become scarce on Cape Cod. Virtually all rosy red finches are House Finches. House Finches are common at feeders and nest in houseplants, porch lights, signs, and so forth. This is because they are an introduced species and have no natural nesting niche in the eastern U.S. Males show rosy red of varying degrees, depending on age. Females are brown and finely streaked.

ORIOLES & FINCHES

American Goldfinch

5″
(year round)

Very common. This yellow, black, and white finch fools a lot of people. Adult male in breeding plumage is easy to identify—black cap, black wings, and black tail with bright yellow throat, breast, back, and belly. At feeders, any olive green, yellowish finch with two white wing bars is a goldfinch in non-breeding plumage. This "wild canary" sings as it flies in a deeply undulating pattern.

6"
(year round)

House Sparrow

Preferred habitat is residential neighborhoods and fast-food-restaurant parking lots. Male has a black bib and gray crown. Female is brown with white eye stripe.

This is not a sparrow, but actually a Eurasian weaver finch introduced to the United States in the late nineteenth century.

BIRDINGTOURS
on Cape Cod

The following tours are designed to help the beginning or novice birder become familiar with a variety of habitats on Cape Cod and the common birds that are associated with them, whether on spring or fall migration, summer nesting grounds, or during the non-breeding, typically fall and winter months. While these tours offer suggestions as to what species will be encountered and how to identify them, always look for more!

Birding Cape Cod, published by The Massachusetts Audubon Society and the Cape Cod Bird Club is an excellent book that will lead you to many super birding spots on the Cape and Islands.

Birds of the Woodlands
Spring and Summer

One of the most exciting times to watch birds is during their spring migration. Most birds are in their breeding plumage, the weather is pleasantly warm, and the birds often move through in waves providing great opportunities to look at numbers of birds. Birds, such as warblers, vireos, sparrows, swallows, and finches, are active, brightly colored, and sing jubilantly in the spring. A number of these species nest on the Cape and can be observed through the month of July and even into August.

Almost any pine-oak forest will produce birds, but a few areas stand out as birding hot-spots:

The Beech Forest in Provincetown

Wellfleet Bay Wildlife Sanctuary in South Wellfleet

Lowell Holly Reservation in Mashpee

These are areas that provide food, shelter, and water for spring migrants and nesting species. As you bird these areas in spring and throughout the year, look and listen for birds high and low. You may not be able to identify a bird by its song at first; but, once

you see a warbler or sparrow throw its head back, point its beak to the sky, and let go a chorus, you will be able to associate that bird with its song forever.

Three common species of woodland warblers are the **Black-and-white Warbler**, the **Pine Warbler**, and the **Ovenbird**. The Black-and-white Warbler is vivid and boldly patterned; the Pine Warbler and the Ovenbird are fairly drab and seldom seen. The Pine Warbler sings from high in the Pitch Pines and the Ovenbird stays hidden in the woodland floor undergrowth yet their songs ring out loudly in the spring air. Although you will hear the Pine Warbler sing its monotonic trill from high up in the pitch pines, finding this little pale yellow warbler may not be easy. The Ovenbird is a hard-to-find resident of the forest floor. Its song, steadily rising in volume, sounds like *teacher, teacher, teacher, teacher, teacher.* Just when you think you've walked close enough to see it, the song will start up behind you!

Another secretive bird, the **Red-eyed Vireo**, spends its days in treetops and sings short, musical phrases over and over again.

Several species of birds that have visited feeders over the winter months also occupy the woodlands in spring. **The Tufted Titmouse, Black-capped Chickadee, White-breasted Nuthatch,** and **Downy Woodpecker** all nest on the Cape.

Along the woodland edge listen for the bubbly, gurgling phrases of the **Gray Catbird**. This mimic, which is gray with a black cap, is familiar in yards and gardens. The brilliant **Yellow Warbler** is found along all edge habitats, especially near water. The hard-to-see but very vocal common **Yellowthroat** sings *wichity wichity wichity,* always close to the ground, in dense undergrowth. This tiny warbler, greenish with a bright yellow throat and black face mask, nests over the entire Cape.

When the woodland borders a pond or lake, a greater variety of birds may be found. The **Eastern Phoebe** is a flycatcher, as is the **Eastern Kingbird**. Both sit on bare branches over or near water; they flit off to catch an insect and then return to perch. The phoebe is olive-green/gray above (with no wing bars), and is pale below. It has a distinct habit of pumping its tail up and down. The call is a nasal *fee-bee*. The Eastern Kingbird is unmistakable; it is jet black above and pure white below with a white band at the tip of the tail. Kingbirds have an affinity for perching on the edge of a Pitch Pine branch over a pond or marsh.

Look also for swallows skimming over the surface of the pond. Both the **Tree Swallow** and the **Barn Swallow** eat thousands of mosquitoes and other flying insects each day. The brilliant blue back of the Tree Swallow and the deeply forked tail of the Barn Swallow are field marks that confirm identification of these fast-flying insect eaters. Tree Swallows may be seen in the hundreds on any spring or summer day. As you scan with binoculars, look for both the **Bank Swallow**, brown with a dark band across the chest, and the smaller **Rough-winged Swallow**, brown above and paler below.

In woodland meadows or adjacent fields, especially where Eastern Red Cedar or Pitch Pine are prevalent, look and listen for the **Prairie Warbler**. This tiny warbler is often heard before it is seen. Listen for a rapid series of notes rising in pitch. Along almost any back dune area, especially on the Outer Cape, where bayberry is growing in the dunes or beach grass habitat, Prairie Warblers should be listened for; remember, they sing from low branches and move from one perch to another within the boundaries of their nesting territory.

Another bird that sings from bush tops is the **Song Sparrow**. This is the common sparrow of the Cape and is found everywhere. It is brown above and pale below. It has heavy brown streaks on the breast that form a dark center spot. Song Sparrow territories overlap throughout yards, meadows, and wood edges.

Not as numerous, but nesting and living close to the ground in the Scrub Oak thickets is the **Eastern Towhee**. Towhees rustle the leaves with a two-footed shuffle, as they look for insects and grubs, the insects' larvae. Towhees give two distinct songs: *chew-wink* and *drink-your-teeeee*. Either call will give away the presence of this secretive black, white, and chestnut-colored relative of the sparrow.

Songbirds are everywhere during June and July! On some days, when all conditions are perfect for migration, the numbers of birds and their variety may seem overwhelming to both the casual and experienced bird-watcher.

Remember to take your time as you look through binoculars. You won't see every bird, but begin by locating the bird near distinct twigs, branch forks, a flower, or anything that will put you onto the bird. Look at every bird you see, whether sitting swimming, or even flying, it is all good practice. You'll get better every time out!

Waterfowl of Freshwater Lakes and Ponds

The great variety of lakes, ponds, and marshes on the Cape provides shelter and food for many species of ducks and other waterfowl. Shallow vegetated ponds and creeks attract dabbling ducks, Canada Geese, and the Mute Swan, while the deeper ponds attract the diving ducks. Any season will provide the birding enthusiast with good views of ducks, but, generally, fall, winter, and spring are best for observing a diversity of species. Although many duck species are present in summer, most ducks are rather rare at this season and tend to be secretive, as nesting is under way. Also, most have molted into a dull brown non-breeding, or eclipse, plumage and remain this way until the fall when they take on the breeding plumage of the upcoming spring.

From November through April, we see the best variety and the greatest number of freshwater ducks on the Cape and Islands. Several ponds stand out as hot-spots, predictable sources for waterfowl viewing. They are:

Siders Pond and Salt Pond in the center of Falmouth

The Mill Pond at the intersection of Rt. 149 and Rt. 28 in Marston's Mills

Hallets Mill Pond, off Route 6A in Cummaquid, Barnstable

Walker's Pond on Slough Road, Brewster

Cliff Pond in Nickerson State Park, Brewster

Lovers Lake in Chatham

Great Pond in Eastham

Herring Pond in Eastham

These ponds will usually have several species present and, in combination, could provide many of the freshwater species possible on the Cape.

A number of species, especially the diving ducks and mergansers, may appear in saltwater estuaries or tidal creeks, especially when ponds and lakes are frozen. The two most common ducks to be found on the Cape and Islands are the **Mallard** (easily identified by its green head, white neck ring, rusty breast, and yellow bill), and the **Black Duck** (actually very dark brown with a paler brown head and with a dull, mustard yellow bill). The two are often together and do interbreed. The female Mallard is brown overall, lighter than the Black Duck, and has an orange bill. The Mallard is an introduced species and may ultimately cause the extinction of the pure Black Duck through interbreeding.

A stately looking duck is the **Northern Pintail**, named for its long black tail feathers. The Pintail's chocolate brown head contrasts with its white neck and breast; a single white stripe extends up the side of the head. Females are light brown overall and may be identified by their noticeably long, thin neck.

Another handsome duck is the **American Wigeon**. This is a duck with a gray head with green strip through the eye, and a white cap and forehead help to identify this handsome drake (male). Females are brown with a gray head and rusty sides. All of these ducks are dabblers—they feed in shallow water by tipping up to reach vegetation.

Two more dabbler species, very small in comparison to the others, are the **Blue-winged Teal** and **Green-winged Teal**. Both are easily identified by their head pattern and small size. The Green-winged Teal, the more common of the two, is the smallest dabbler and has a chestnut-colored head with a green ear patch. The Blue-winged Teal has a bluish gray head with a striking white crescent between the bill and the eye. The females of both species are small and brown. Think of the name of the species as you notice the green or blue wing patches. It will help you identify the female teals.

Sometimes we observe a group of ducks flying by at a distance. Whether in a large flock or a few birds, the teal will stand out because of their small size.

Two species of dabbling ducks that are less common, but should be looked for, are the **Gadwall** and the **Northern Shoveler**. The Gadwall may be hard to identify because of its nondescript coloration. The male appears mostly gray, but look for the black tail area and the small white patch on the wing. Females resemble female Mallards but have the white wing patch and are a bit smaller. A good spot to find Gadwalls during the winter is Mill Pond at the intersection of Routes 149 and 28 in Marstons Mills, Barnstable. The Shoveler's huge, spatulate bill and chestnut, green, and white plumage should help to identify this uncommon duck.

Two species of large waterfowl occur on freshwater ponds, the **Canada Goose** and the **Mute Swan** (an introduced species).

Of the diving ducks found in freshwater ponds and lakes, the **Bufflehead** is the most common. Equally at home in fresh or salt water, this small diver often forms large flocks and is widespread.

The **Ring-necked Duck** and the two species of scaup are also common diving ducks. The **Greater Scaup** and **Lesser Scaup** are so difficult to separate in the field that even experts simply refer to them as scaup species. Both are dark-fronted with white sides and gray backs. Females appear brown overall with a broad white patch at the base of the bill. The Ring-necked Duck has the same overall pattern as the scaup, but has a white ring close to the bill tip and a noticeable white vertical flash between the breast and sides.

Don't be afraid to come to a conclusion on the identification of any bird you see. Cover as many field marks as you can, starting with the head pattern and remember that it's okay to let one get away.

Also look for the small **Ruddy Duck** with its white cheeks, dark cap, and characteristically cocked tail.

Two uncommon diving ducks are the **Canvasback** and the **Redhead**. Both have a chestnut head, black breast, and grayish sides but are easily separated by head profile: the Canvasback has a long, sloping forehead and beak. With both of these species, which are uncommon but may be seen in ones and twos at various locations, the females are patterned similarly to the males but duller overall.

Another large freshwater duck with a rusty-reddish head is the **American, or Common, Merganser**. This is a stately bird with bright, white sides and a green head, highlighted by a bright red bill. The drake, described here, is easily recognized, not only by its white sides, but by its large size. Although they are not often encountered, Common Mergansers may be seen on ponds, lakes, or bays anytime after early November. The female is handsome in her own right, showing a rusty red body and head with a white throat and patch on the wing.

The **Hooded Mergansers** is a flamboyant little duck with a brightly contrasting hood of black and white, a white breast with vertical black stripes, and rusty sides. This handsome bird is unmistakable in the field. Like the Common Merganser, the female is rusty in plumage overall.

Two species of waterfowl often encountered in fresh water that are not in the duck family are the **Pied-billed Grebe** and the **American Coot**. Both are easy to identify. The Pied-billed Grebe is brown and tiny, smaller even than the Bufflehead; it has a stout, pointed bill. Often seen near pond edges, the little "hell-diver" can disappear beneath the surface without a ripple. The American Coot is dark gray overall with a distinct, white bill. It feeds both by dabbling and diving.

Twenty-one species of freshwater ducks and waterfowl are mentioned here. This may seem like a lot, but, by watching and separating the dabblers from the divers, the choices are narrowed considerably. Any of these species may be encountered by visiting the ponds mentioned above or your own favorite pond, so take your time and have fun!

Common Birds of the Salt Marsh

Around much of the perimeter of Cape Cod is a fringe of green. This area, situated behind the protective dunes and at the foot of the gently sloping upland, is calm, open, often expansive, and wet grassland. This is the salt marsh. Influenced by every tide, it is rich in life and in life-sustaining nutrients. Salt marshes of Cape Cod may be huge, such as the marsh in Barnstable and the marsh at Nauset. Others may only be small patches of the marsh grass Spartina.

Birds can be found in the salt marsh during any season. In some cases, it's possible to walk in the marsh; in others, it is better to scan the marsh with the binoculars or spotting scope to find its avian inhabitants. Winter is the quietest season. The period between May and October will produce the greatest number and variety of birds, both nesting species and migrants.

The salt marsh in winter appears brown, bleak, cold, and wind-blown. It is all of these. Only the hardiest birds inhabit its flooded creeks. Most common of these is the **Black Duck**. A solid-colored, dark brown dabbler or puddle duck, it is virtually the only dabbler found abundantly in salt water. **Canada Geese** flock in the marsh to feed and roost, both in the high marsh and along its watery edge.

Along the creek edges a long-legged **Great Blue Heron** may linger, while two species of diving ducks, the **Red-breasted Merganser** and the **Bufflehead**, chase the same mummichogs that are hunted stealthily by the wading heron. The **Red-breasted Merganser**, which also

frequents the open seas, is easily identified by its dark green head, white neck ring, and conspicuous crest. Females have the same crested shape, but appear reddish-brown overall. The **Bufflehead**, a small duck, is black and white. Most obvious on the male is a bold white head patch over most of the crown. The female is dark overall with a small white patch behind the eye.

Look for the **Northern Harrier** (or Marsh Hawk) low over the salt marsh as it courses to hunt for ducks, or look along the marsh edges as it searches for its favorite prey, the Meadow Vole. The white rump patch immediately identifies this long-winged hawk.

During April and May a steady stream of migrants arrives at the salt marsh. First to be seen and heard is the **Red-winged Blackbird**. Bright red-and-yellow shoulder patches identify this blackbird, which will nest along the marsh edge and remain until fall.

The **Laughing Gull** is our only black-headed gull. This loud, crow-sized gull feeds in the high marsh, along the edges of open sea or bay.

Throughout the warm months, look for the **Snowy Egret**. Widespread in the Cape's salt marshes, this is the white egret of the marsh. Black bill, black legs, and yellow feet help to identify it.

Another heron, small and dark, stands motionless at the edge of the marsh—the **Green Heron**, usually found in the fresher or brackish areas of the marsh.

Anyone who is in the vicinity of a salt marsh at dusk or after dark may hear the call of the **Black-crowned Night Herons**. These stocky herons, gray and white with a black cap, call *kwok.....kwok*, as they fly overhead, often in twos and threes, as they leave their daytime roost to forage in the marsh at night.

Some birds may be difficult to observe in the tall marsh grass. The **Willet** (a large sandpiper) and the **Saltmarsh Sharp-tailed Sparrow** may be seen flying over the salt marsh and may be identified readily by their behavior. Both birds nest in proximity to the salt marsh. The Willet calls a loud *wi-wi-llet, wi-wi-llet, wi-wi-llet* incessantly as it swoops past any intruder on the marsh and flashes its bright white wing patches. The tiny Saltmarsh Sharp-tailed Sparrow is more subtle. Its ochre-colored face patch is not easily seen as it quickly jumps from the grass, flies along 15-20 feet at grass height, then drops, and disappears. The jump-and-drop behavior of this very secretive sparrow helps to identify it.

All through the warm months, swallows zig-zag over the marsh to catch insects on the wing. **Tree Swallows** and **Barn Swallows** are most common.

Common Terns and **Least Terns** hover over marsh creeks and dive for small fish. Although these two gray-and-white, black-capped seabirds are seen more commonly along the seashore, they often follow the rising tide into the salt marsh.

Another bird that hovers and dives for fish is the **Belted Kingfisher**. Usually before the Kingfisher is seen, its long, rattling call echoes across the marsh. This crested, blue-and-white fisher perches nearby at the water's edge.

As the nesting season wanes, fall migrants begin to appear along the Cape's shoreline. Most of these are shorebirds—sandpipers and plovers. A few, most notably the tiny **Least Sandpiper**, prefer the muddy creek edges of the salt marsh. **Willets**, though still in the marsh, are much less noisy with no nest to protect. Small flocks of **Greater Yellowlegs** stand in shallow water. **Snowy Egrets**, often in sizable flocks, prepare to head south. Flocks of **Black-bellied Plovers** often rest in the marsh while the larger **Whimbrel**, with its striped head and strongly de-curved bill, forages for Fiddler Crabs and plucks them from their burrows in the salt marsh hay.

All of Cape Cod's habitats support bird populations. By visiting certain habitats, we often encounter predictable bird species. The salt marsh is one of the many habitats where the bird-watcher can predict, find, and identify species easily. So get out there with binoculars and find all the species mentioned here. They're all there and waiting.

Shorebirds of the Tidal Flats
in late Summer

It's late summer, a time when shorebirds are at the peak of their southward migration over Cape Cod. These birds have completed their nesting season in the far north and are making their way to the southern United States and South America for the winter. They begin to appear along our shores in early July, and although some may linger into the winter months, most will have headed south over the Atlantic by late September.

The term shorebirds is the collective name for sandpipers, plovers, oystercatchers, and their allies. A good variety is here in late July and August. It is easier than you may think to sort them out and identify them.

Find the **American Oystercatchers** first. They stand out from all the other birds because of their size, contrasting plumage, and bright orange bill. One of the largest shorebirds, these black, brown, and white shellfish eaters are often found on the mussel beds.

Two other large shorebirds of the tidal flats are the **Willet** and the **Greater Yellowlegs**. Both are sandpipers. In flight, the Willet is unmistakable with its large, flashy, white wing patches. At rest this gray, nondescript shorebird with dull gray legs stands almost as tall as the oystercatchers. Listen for the Willet's call—a loud *wi-wi-llett, wi-wi-llett*—repeated again and again. The Greater Yellowlegs stands almost as tall as the Willet,

but it appears more slender and has bright yellow legs, an unmistakable field mark. Both the Willet and Greater Yellowlegs have a relatively long bill and long legs.

Not as common, the **Lesser Yellowlegs** is nearly identical in plumage to the Greater, but it is smaller, with a thin, petite bill. Rather than the loud, clear three-note call of the Greater Yellowlegs, the lesser has a thinner two-note call when it takes flight. The majority of Yellowlegs seen are Greater Yellowlegs, but it's worth taking a second look.

Next, look for a shorter, chunky sandpiper with a very long bill. Its reddish brown plumage and bold white eye stripe identify it as a **Short-billed Dowitcher**. True, this bird has a very long bill, but it is not the rare **Long-billed Dowitcher,** which prefers non-tidal habitats. All dowitchers show a white flash up the middle of the back in flight, look for it as they fly by.

Two types of plovers are probably here, the **Semipalmated Plover** and the **Black-bellied Plover**. The Semipalmated Plover is small, rich dark brown above and white below, and has a dark ring around its neck. They may be here in large numbers. So may the Black-bellied Plover. If it is in breeding plumage, it is easy to identify: black below, white on the sides of its neck and breast, and mottled black and white on its back. Remember, though, in non-breeding

plumage it is a nondescript, mottled brown and white. Its relatively stout, black bill will help to identify this, the only common large plover of the tidal flats.

Now find the **Ruddy Turnstone**, the calico cat of the bird world. This rusty brown, black, and white bird with orange legs looks like a cross between a sandpiper and a plover. It is often seen foraging along the sandy shores at the edge of the tidal flats, flipping shells, vegetation, or pebbles, true to its name.

The last of the robin-sized birds to be found on these tidal flats is the **Red Knot.** It is gray on the back, brick red (bright or dull) below, and has short legs and a short bill. Although you may often find Red Knots in groups feeding with Dowitchers, you should not confuse the two species if you note the obvious differences in bill length.

Now focus your binoculars on the smallest sandpipers. Four sparrow-sized species may be found.

The **Sanderling** is the largest of these and appears in a variety of plumages, depending on its sex and age. In spring through late summer, the Sanderling appears chestnut (bright or dull) above and white below. Later in the season the Sanderling molts to a pearly gray above and white below. The bill is rather short and black.

Similar in size to the Sanderling, but darker gray on the back and with a long bill that seems to droop at the tip, is the **Dunlin**. Dunlins often winter over on the cape and during the cold windswept days of December and January, Dunlins and Sanderlings may be seen on the tidal flats, foraging for whatever they can find to eat. When seen on spring migration, the Dunlin is a rich chestnut above and pale below with a distinct black patch on the breast and belly.

As we continue scanning the flats we see the **Semipalmated Sandpiper**, probably the most abundant of all the shorebirds observed. It is small, dull, brownish gray above and streaked and pale below, with a black bill. They seem to run around everywhere. Note the black legs of the Semipalmated Sandpiper in contrast to the next small species.

The **Least Sandpiper** is tiny. Best identified by its smallest size and pale, drab yellow legs, "leasties" are usually found near the grassy edges of the tidal flats.

There! You've made it through the most common shorebirds found on the Cape and Islands! Almost any tidal flats from Provincetown to Martha's Vineyard will offer a variety of migrant shorebirds. Be patient, sort them out, have fun

Migrants on Salt Water

In late autumn, when cold winds blow hard from the northwest, up to twenty-five species of ducks can be seen in Cape Cod waters. Some duck species occur primarily on the open seas, some prefer saltwater bays and rivers, and others prefer the habitat of freshwater ponds and lakes.

Let us first visit the open waters of Cape Cod Bay. Many locations on the bay will provide good news of wintering and migrating ducks, as well as views of loons, grebes, gulls, and gannets. Four of the choicest locations are:

Sandy Neck Beach in Barnstable

Corporation Beach in Dennis

First Encounter Beach in Eastham

Herring Cove Beach, Provincetown.

All these places provide an opportunity to view the open water from your parked car. To see some birds that may be well offshore, it is helpful to use a spotting scope. At any location along the outer beaches of the cape in winter the enthusiastic birder is likely turn up many of these species of ducks. Only Nantucket Sound may show a lower diversity of species.

All sea ducks dive beneath the surface to feed on fish or mollusks or vegetation. Look first for the **Common Eider**. The Common Eider is white on the face, neck, breast and back, black on the cap, sides and tail. You'll notice on closer inspection, a subtle greenish-yellow tinge to the nape. This is a black-and-white duck; in fact, it

is the biggest duck you will see. Often seen in floating flocks, called rafts, the black-capped, white-faced males are accompanied by the chestnut brown females and mottled brown-and-white immature males. In flight, eiders (like most sea ducks), fly low over the water in wavy lines.

Three species of scoters may be seen on the winter seas. The males are all quite distinctive. **The Black Scoter**, smallest of the three, is all-black with an orange knob on the bill. The **Surf Scoter** is also black but shows a white patch on the forehead and nape, hence the nickname skunk-head. The third and largest scoter is the **White-winged Scoter**. It is all black, but for a white comma-shaped patch over the eye and a white wing patch visible on the side as it swims and clearly visible on the wing in flight against an all black body. Females of all three species are a dull brown and can be difficult to identify at a distance. Female Black Scoters show a pale cheek and throat contrasting with a darker cap. Female Surf Scoters may show dull white face patches. The female White-winged Scoter also shows dull face patches and may show a white wing patch when swimming. If a scoter shows a white wing patch while swimming or in flight, it is a White-winged Scoter. All three species of scoters and the Common Eider often form rafts of hundreds, or even thousands, of birds. So the appearance of large numbers does not necessarily mean a great variety of species.

Another very widespread, often numerous, duck is the **Red-breasted Merganser**. Separate this species from the previous four by its long-necked, streamlined shape, especially in flight. Males have a dark green, crested head and broad white neck ring. Females are reddish brown on the crest, head, and neck. Both sexes show prominent white wing patches in flight, but shouldn't be confused with scoters. Scoters appear "chunky" while the Red-breasted Merganser is long-bodied.

Bufflehead and **Common Goldeneye** have wing patches also, but are chunky and smaller and show white face patches. They are found in the open waters of Cape Cod Bay only during migration.

Keep an eye out for the brown-winged, white-bodied **Oldsquaw** to dart by. This small sea duck has a distinctive brown band across its white breast.

Two species of loons may be encountered. Look for the **Common Loon**, which is blackish above, with a white cheek, throat and breast. Also note the dagger-like bill. The Common Loon is larger than the largest ducks. The **Red-throated Loon** is smaller and grayer than the Common Loon with a thin pointed bill that appears upturned. Remembering that loons occur singly will help you separate them from ducks.

The **Horned Grebe**, small and compact, has the same dark-above/white-below pattern and is usually solitary. But remember, it is very small and appears square-headed.

During the winter months the **Brant**, a stocky, black-necked goose, is often found in the grassy beach edges of the bay. Compared to the **Canada Goose**, the other possibility, the Brant is smaller, lacks a white cheek but has a white patch on the neck and is black on the breast (the Canada Goose has a pale breast).

Gulls may be observed constantly. Our common gray **Herring Gull** and the larger **Great Black-backed Gull** are ever present and may be observed year round. In late November, look for the tiny **Bonaparte's Gull** flying by. Only half the size of the Herring Gull and often appearing in small flocks, this gray-and-white gull shows a distinctive white flash in the primaries at the end of the wing, a petite black bill, and a black spot behind the eye. The **Iceland Gull** is a winter visitor and may be observed along the outer beach, in the company of Herring Gulls and Great Black-backed Gulls. Iceland Gulls often appear uniformly white and are close to the size of a Herring Gull, but a bit smaller. When looking at gulls along the winter beaches, always look for the "white-winged gull."

Northern Gannets may be observed on some days, especially when there are north or northeast winds. Adult gannets are pure white with black wing tips. Juvenile and immature birds are dark brown or mottled brown and white, but are the size of the adults. Gannets are very big, larger than any gull, and appear pointed at the head, tail and wings. They dive like rockets into the sea to feed on fish and squid.

Although the diversity of species is often low in Cape Cod Bay during the winter, with only a few species represented, the bay will often be teeming with several thousand birds. Look at them all and sort them out. Have fun!

Oceanic Birds

Almost every visitor to Cape Cod who has an interest in nature eventually goes on a whale watch. Good-sized, comfortable boats leave from Plymouth, Barnstable, and Provincetown every day in summer for the same destination, an underwater mound north of Provincetown called Stellwagen Bank. There, a rapid change in sea depth, water temperature, and salinity brings about a great diversity of marine organisms, from microscopic plankton to immense schools of fish, to the massive whales which are at the top of the food chain.

On such a sea trip, the amateur naturalist and bird-watcher is given the opportunity to observe some of the most fascinating avian life on our planet, the free-roaming pelagic seabirds, most notably shearwaters and storm-petrels. Most of the seabirds that are seen by us during our summer (but actually their winter) are thousands of miles from the islands in the South Atlantic and Antarctic regions where they nest. On some days, shearwaters and storm-petrels may appear in the thousands, while on other days they are absent altogether.

Wilson's Storm-petrel is the only species of storm-petrel that is normally observed on whale watches. The other possibility, **Leach's Storm-petrel**, is very rarely seen on Stellwagen Bank. Wilson's is the storm-petrel that we commonly see offshore. Three species of shearwaters: the **Great Shearwater**, the **Sooty Shearwater**, and the less common **Manx Shearwater**, are all a pretty good bet during the late summer and fall. The largest of our shearwaters is the **Cory's Shearwater**. This pale brown above, light below species has a distinctive yellow bill and no rump patch. It is a northern hemisphere nester and flies across and around the North Atlantic Ocean, unlike its cousin the Great Shearwater, which migrates across the equator from Antarctic realms.

As you leave the inner harbor, whether it be Plymouth, Barnstable, or Provincetown, look for **Double-crested Cormorants** on rocks or pilings. These upright-standing black birds with orange bills are often observed with wings spread as they stand in the sun.

The **Herring Gull**, our common gray-and-white gull, is everywhere, as is the larger, but less numerous, **Great Black-backed Gull**. Immatures of both species are a mottled brown and remain so for two and three years respectively.

If you head north out over the open water toward Stellwagen Bank, you will see numbers of terns. These are almost certainly all **Common Terns**, but the **Roseate Tern**, now federally endangered, may be seen. The two species are more easily identified by call. Although they differ slightly in color, their calls are quite different. Listen for the nasal *chi-vik, chi-vik, chi-vik* of the Roseate Tern and the Common Tern's harsh *kee-er kee-eer* call. Listen carefully—you might find a Roseate Tern or two. Both are graceful, fork-tailed, gray-and-white seabirds with long pointed wings and a black cap. Roseates are more silvery on the upper parts and have long, streaming, white tail feathers. The Common Tern is grayer and has a forked tail with black on the outer edges.

The **Least Tern** is much smaller than either the Common or Roseate Tern. Most notable is its short tail and tiny size. The call is a high-pitched squeaky *ki-dik ki-dee, ki-dik ki-dee*. Least Terns, like the common and roseates, hover and dive for fish all day long. Look for these birds as you leave or enter harbors.

Most people on the boat are looking for spouts. Suddenly a small, black bird flies past the bow, close to the water, a **Wilson's Storm-petrel**. This bird is all black, is about the size of a cardinal, and has a white rump patch. Wilson's Storm-petrels patter over the surface when they feed. Keep watch for the **Sooty Shearwater** and **Great Shearwater**, crow-sized birds with long, stiff wings. The Sooty Shearwater is unmistakable; it is a dark chocolate brown all over, with silvery under-wings or wing linings. The Great Shearwater is a bit larger; it is brown above and has a dark black cap, a pale collar, a white breast, and a white rump patch. You might also notice the brown belly smudge. Both shearwaters fly fast and alternate several flaps with a water-shearing glide.

A smaller shearwater is the **Manx Shearwater**, less common (usually) than the two previous species and almost half their size. Manx Shearwaters have no white rump patch and are dark brown (almost black) above and pure white below. They have the same shape and characteristics as the other shearwaters, but the Manx is smaller and usually solitary.

Look also for the **Parasitic Jaeger** (yay,ger). It is gull-like and dark brown above with creamy pale undersides. The mark to look for is the white flash near the top of each wing. Jaegers are kleptoparasites, that is, they live by stealing food, most often from terns. So watch for the chase, one of the birds may be a jaeger, but do not be confused by immature **Laughing Gulls**, which are very common offshore.

One other pelagic bird to seek is the rare **Northern Fulmar**, which is a special treat to observe. This bird (not mentioned earlier) has the same color pattern as the Herring Gull (white head and underparts with a pale gray back and upper wings) but differs in shape and flight. Fulmars look like a stocky shearwater and fly with stiff wings and a rapid wing beat. They're tough to find but don't count them out!

Whale-watching trips provide an excellent opportunity to see oceanic birds that are rarely seen otherwise. The ocean is a big place with lots of room, so don't be discouraged if you see very few birds. Sometimes you will see thousands of birds; sometimes, none. In late summer or fall, it's tough to miss seeing some birds.

Remember, look at every bird and have fun!

: NO ILLUSTRATION